Mastering JavaScript Frameworks: From React to Angular

A Complete Guide to JavaScript Frameworks for Building Web Apps

BOOZMAN RICHARD

BOOKER BLUNT

Table of Content

TABLE OF CONTENTS

4

5

INTRODUCTION

Mastering JavaScript Frameworks: From React to Angular

The web development landscape has evolved dramatically over the past decade, with JavaScript frameworks playing a pivotal role in shaping how developers build interactive, dynamic, and scalable applications. In this rapidly changing ecosystem, staying up to date with the latest frameworks and technologies is crucial to building high-performance web applications that meet user expectations for speed, reliability, and seamless experiences across devices.

This book, *Mastering JavaScript Frameworks: From React to Angular*, is designed to be your comprehensive guide to mastering the most popular JavaScript frameworks used in modern web development. Whether you are just starting your journey into web development or you're a seasoned developer looking to deepen your knowledge, this book covers everything you need to know about **React**, **Angular**, and **Vue.js**. Each chapter is crafted to provide you with a clear understanding of the core concepts, best practices, and real-world examples, helping you build scalable, maintainable, and performant applications.

Why This Book Is Essential

The demand for rich, interactive web applications has never been higher. With the rise of Single Page Applications (SPAs), Progressive Web Apps (PWAs), and mobile-first design, developers must not only understand the principles of front-end development but also leverage modern JavaScript frameworks to enhance the user experience and meet the growing demands of today's digital world.

In this book, you will:

- Gain a deep understanding of **React**, **Angular**, and **Vue.js**, each of which has its unique strengths and weaknesses.
- Learn how to implement best practices for building fast, efficient, and secure web applications.
- Dive into advanced topics such as **state management**, **routing**, **service workers**, and **performance optimization**.
- Explore real-world examples of building web apps from scratch, including integrating APIs, securing user data, and optimizing performance.

- Get hands-on experience with building **Progressive Web Apps (PWAs), Single Page Applications (SPAs)**, and mobile-first web solutions.

Whether you're looking to improve your skills in building scalable front-end applications or need to stay updated with the latest trends and technologies in web development, this book will serve as your essential companion.

What You Will Learn

In the first part of the book, we'll explore the foundational concepts of JavaScript frameworks. You'll get acquainted with the core principles behind **React**, **Angular**, and **Vue.js**, including their strengths, weaknesses, and appropriate use cases. We'll dive into the fundamentals of each framework, helping you choose the right tool for your next project.

Next, we will cover how to build real-world applications with these frameworks. You'll learn how to develop powerful web apps by creating dynamic user interfaces, managing state effectively, and implementing modern features like **routing**, **authentication**, and **data binding**. You'll also get hands-on experience building **single-page**

applications (SPAs) and integrating APIs to enhance the functionality of your app.

As we move deeper into advanced topics, the book will guide you through **state management** using libraries like **Redux** for React, **NgRx** for Angular, and **Vuex** for Vue.js. We'll also focus on performance optimization techniques such as **code splitting**, **lazy loading**, **caching**, and **progressive web apps (PWAs)** to ensure that your web apps perform at their best across all devices and network conditions.

Security is also a major concern when developing web applications. In this book, we'll explore how to protect your app from common vulnerabilities like **Cross-Site Scripting (XSS)**, **Cross-Site Request Forgery (CSRF)**, and **SQL Injection**. You'll learn how to implement secure authentication systems using **JWT** (JSON Web Tokens) and other modern techniques to safeguard your app's data and user privacy.

The final section of the book covers best practices and strategies for maintaining and evolving your web apps. We'll focus on **test-driven development (TDD)**, **unit testing**, and **end-to-end testing** with tools like **Jest**, **Karma**, and **Protractor**. We'll also discuss how to stay up to date with the latest trends and frameworks in the JavaScript ecosystem, ensuring your skills remain relevant in the ever-changing world of web development.

Who This Book Is For

This book is intended for developers of all experience levels who want to master modern JavaScript frameworks. Whether you are:

- A **beginner** looking to get started with React, Angular, or Vue.js, and want to learn the fundamentals of web development with modern frameworks.
- An **intermediate developer** who wants to deepen your understanding of state management, routing, testing, and performance optimization.
- An **experienced developer** seeking to stay updated on the latest tools, best practices, and trends in JavaScript frameworks, and how to build scalable, secure, and high-performance web applications.

Why React, Angular, and Vue.js?

The three frameworks covered in this book—**React**, **Angular**, and **Vue.js**—are the most widely used and popular choices for building web applications today. Each framework has unique features, and understanding their strengths and use cases will help you choose the right one for your project.

- **React**: Known for its simplicity and flexibility, React is a **JavaScript library** for building user interfaces. Its component-based architecture and virtual DOM make it highly efficient for rendering dynamic UIs, and it is widely adopted for creating modern, fast web applications.
- **Angular**: Angular is a **full-fledged framework** that provides everything you need for building large-scale web applications. With built-in tools like **dependency injection**, **routing**, and **forms management**, Angular is perfect for building complex, enterprise-level apps.
- **Vue.js**: Vue is a **progressive framework** that is both easy to learn and flexible enough to scale for large applications. It combines the best features of both React and Angular, offering an approachable

learning curve with powerful tools for building dynamic, modern web apps.

By the end of this book, you'll have a solid understanding of these frameworks and the ability to build robust, production-ready web apps with them.

Conclusion

The world of JavaScript frameworks is constantly evolving, and staying up-to-date with the latest tools and techniques is essential for becoming a proficient web developer. *Mastering JavaScript Frameworks: From React to Angular* offers a detailed, hands-on guide to building modern web applications that are fast, scalable, and secure. By mastering these frameworks, you'll be equipped to tackle any web development challenge and stay at the forefront of the ever-changing landscape of web technologies.

Whether you're building a personal project or working on an enterprise-level application, the skills and knowledge you gain from this book will serve as a solid foundation for your future web development career. Let's dive in and explore the power of **React**, **Angular**, and **Vue.js**, and start building modern web apps that users love!

CHAPTER 1

INTRODUCTION TO JAVASCRIPT FRAMEWORKS

Understanding the Role of JavaScript Frameworks in Web Development

JavaScript frameworks have become an integral part of modern web development. At their core, these frameworks provide a structured way to build dynamic and interactive web applications. Unlike vanilla JavaScript, which is often used for smaller scripts and simpler websites, frameworks offer predefined solutions for common tasks, making it easier for developers to create large-scale, feature-rich applications.

In traditional web development, building an application from scratch requires writing a lot of repetitive and boilerplate code. JavaScript frameworks eliminate much of this repetitive work by providing built-in tools, libraries, and conventions that streamline the process. With a framework, developers can focus more on building unique features for their app, rather than reinventing the wheel with every new project.

Why Frameworks Are Crucial for Building Scalable and Maintainable Web Apps

Scalability and maintainability are two of the biggest challenges developers face when building web apps. JavaScript frameworks help address these challenges by enforcing best practices, creating a clean architecture, and providing reusable components that simplify the development process.

- **Scalability**: As applications grow, the complexity of managing data, handling events, and maintaining state increases. Frameworks help by providing tools and patterns that make it easier to scale applications, like component-based architectures and efficient state management systems. These tools help developers keep the app organized and prevent it from becoming too complicated as new features are added.

- **Maintainability**: With a well-organized framework, it's easier to maintain and update an application over time. The modular structure of frameworks ensures that code is divided into smaller, reusable pieces (such as components or services), which makes it easier to modify, test, and debug the app as it evolves. Frameworks also promote consistency across the codebase, which reduces the likelihood of bugs or misunderstandings among team members working on the project.

Additionally, frameworks offer comprehensive documentation, active communities, and third-party tools, which make maintaining and evolving the app more manageable over time.

Overview of Popular JavaScript Frameworks: React, Angular, Vue.js, and More

There are many JavaScript frameworks available, each offering unique features and advantages. Below is an overview of some of the most popular ones:

- **React**: React is a JavaScript library for building user interfaces, developed by Facebook. It's based on a component-driven architecture, where the UI is divided into reusable components that manage their own state. React is known for its fast rendering performance, thanks to its virtual DOM, which minimizes direct manipulation of the browser's DOM. It's primarily used for building single-page applications (SPAs) but can also be used in mobile development via React Native.

- **Angular**: Angular is a full-fledged front-end framework developed by Google. Unlike React, which focuses solely on the view layer, Angular is a complete solution that includes everything from data binding and dependency injection to routing and forms management. Angular uses

19

a two-way data binding model, which means changes in the UI are automatically reflected in the data and vice versa. Angular is often favored for larger, enterprise-level applications because of its scalability and robust feature set.

- **Vue.js**: Vue.js is a progressive JavaScript framework that combines elements of both React and Angular. It is designed to be approachable for beginners, but also powerful enough for advanced developers. Vue offers a flexible architecture that can be used for simple single-page applications or complex, large-scale projects. Vue's core library focuses on the view layer, but it's easy to integrate with other libraries or frameworks to handle more complex tasks, like routing and state management.

- **Other Frameworks**: Besides React, Angular, and Vue.js, there are other frameworks such as **Svelte**, **Ember.js**, **Backbone.js**, and **Meteor.js**, each offering specific features or use cases. Svelte, for example, compiles components to highly efficient vanilla JavaScript, reducing the runtime overhead compared to other frameworks.

Choosing the Right Framework for Your Project

Selecting the right JavaScript framework is a critical decision that can impact the development process and the future success of your project. Here are a few key factors to consider when making your choice:

1. **Project Size and Complexity**:
    o For small projects or prototypes, you may want to use a lightweight framework like Vue.js, which is easy to set up and doesn't require much boilerplate code.
    o For large, enterprise-scale applications, Angular or React may be better suited due to their rich ecosystems, scalability, and support for complex features like routing and state management.
2. **Learning Curve**:
    o React has a relatively simple learning curve, especially for developers already familiar with JavaScript. Its component-based structure is easy to grasp and provides immediate feedback when building applications.
    o Angular, on the other hand, has a steeper learning curve, but it offers a more opinionated approach, which can be beneficial for larger teams or more structured development environments.

21

o Vue.js strikes a balance, offering a simpler learning curve than Angular but with more features than React out of the box.

3. **Community and Ecosystem**:

   o React has the largest community and the most mature ecosystem, with numerous libraries, tools, and resources available to help developers.

   o Angular also has strong community support, especially for enterprise applications, while Vue.js has a rapidly growing community and a reputation for being beginner-friendly.

4. **Performance**:

   o React and Vue are known for their excellent performance, especially when rendering complex UIs with many dynamic elements.

   o Angular's performance can be slightly slower due to its two-way data binding, but it's still highly optimized for large-scale applications.

5. **Integration with Other Technologies**:

   o Consider how well the framework integrates with the back-end technologies you plan to use. For instance, React is often used with Node.js and Express for full-stack JavaScript development, while Angular is frequently paired with Java and .NET for enterprise solutions.

Ultimately, the right framework for your project depends on the specific requirements, the scale of the application, and your team's familiarity with the framework. Testing and prototyping with a small application can help clarify the best choice for your needs.

In this chapter, we've introduced the concept of JavaScript frameworks, explained their role in modern web development, and provided an overview of the most popular ones. The next chapter will delve deeper into the core principles of JavaScript that every developer should understand before working with any framework.

CHAPTER 2

JAVASCRIPT FUNDAMENTALS EVERY DEVELOPER SHOULD KNOW

Core JavaScript Concepts: Variables, Functions, Objects, and Arrays

Before diving into JavaScript frameworks like React, Angular, or Vue, it's essential to have a strong grasp of JavaScript's core concepts. These are the building blocks of any web app and will help you understand how frameworks work under the hood.

- **Variables**: Variables are used to store data that can be accessed and modified during the execution of a program. In JavaScript, we use `var`, `let`, and `const` to declare variables.
    - `var` is function-scoped and can be redeclared.
    - `let` is block-scoped and cannot be redeclared in the same scope.
    - `const` is also block-scoped but is used for variables that should not be reassigned.

24

```
javascript
```

```javascript
let name = "John"; // can be reassigned
const age = 30; // cannot be reassigned
```

- **Functions**: Functions allow you to group code into reusable blocks that can be called whenever needed. Functions can accept parameters and return values.

```
javascript
```

```javascript
function greet(name) {
    return "Hello, " + name + "!";
}
console.log(greet("Alice"));  // Outputs:
Hello, Alice!
```

- **Objects**: Objects are collections of key-value pairs where each key is a property and the value is the corresponding data. They are used to represent complex data structures.

```
javascript
```

```javascript
let person = {
    name: "John",
    age: 30,
    greet: function() {
        console.log("Hello,        "        +
this.name);
```

25

```
    }
};
person.greet(); // Outputs: Hello, John
```

- **Arrays**: Arrays are ordered collections of items, which can be of any type, including other arrays and objects. You can access elements in an array by their index.

```javascript
let fruits = ["apple", "banana", "cherry"];
console.log(fruits[1]); // Outputs: banana
```

ES6 Features: Arrow Functions, Promises, Async/Await, Destructuring

JavaScript has evolved significantly with the introduction of ES6 (ECMAScript 2015), bringing new features that make the language more powerful and concise. These features are widely used in modern JavaScript development.

- **Arrow Functions**: Arrow functions provide a shorter syntax for writing functions. They also handle the this keyword differently, making them more intuitive to use in certain contexts, like callbacks and event handlers.

```javascript
```

```
const add = (a, b) => a + b;
console.log(add(2, 3)); // Outputs: 5
```

- **Promises**: Promises are a way to handle asynchronous operations in JavaScript. They represent a value that may not be available yet but will be resolved at some point in the future.

```
javascript

const fetchData = new Promise((resolve,
reject) => {
    let data = true; // Simulating success
    if (data) {
        resolve("Data              fetched
successfully!");
    } else {
        reject("Error fetching data.");
    }
});

fetchData.then(result                    =>
console.log(result)).catch(error          =>
console.log(error));
```

- **Async/Await**: `async` and `await` are syntactic sugar for working with promises. They make asynchronous code look and behave like synchronous code, improving readability and error handling.

27

```
javascript

async function getData() {
    try {
        let    response    =    await
fetch('https://api.example.com/data');
        let data = await response.json();
        console.log(data);
    } catch (error) {
        console.log('Error:', error);
    }
}
getData();
```

- **Destructuring**: Destructuring allows you to extract values from arrays or objects into distinct variables. It can make your code cleaner and more readable.

```
javascript

// Array destructuring
const [first, second] = [1, 2, 3];
console.log(first); // Outputs: 1

// Object destructuring
const person = { name: "John", age: 30 };
const { name, age } = person;
console.log(name); // Outputs: John
```

The DOM and Event Handling in JavaScript

The **Document Object Model (DOM)** is an interface that allows JavaScript to interact with HTML documents. It represents the structure of the page, enabling you to access and manipulate elements such as paragraphs, buttons, images, etc.

- **Selecting Elements**: To interact with elements on a page, you first need to select them. You can use methods like `getElementById()`, `querySelector()`, and `querySelectorAll()`.

javascript

```
let button = document.getElementById('myButton');
let div = document.querySelector('.content');
```

- **Manipulating Elements**: Once you have selected an element, you can modify its properties. For example, you can change the text content or style.

javascript

```
let heading = document.querySelector('h1');
heading.textContent = "Hello, JavaScript!";
```

29

```
heading.style.color = "blue";
```

- **Event Handling**: JavaScript allows you to attach event listeners to elements, so you can respond to user actions like clicks, keypresses, or mouse movements.

```javascript
let button = document.querySelector('button');
button.addEventListener('click', function() {
    alert("Button clicked!");
});
```

This example shows how to listen for a button click and execute a function when the event occurs. JavaScript events play a key role in creating interactive, dynamic web applications.

Real-World Examples: Practical Use Cases of JavaScript in Web Apps

JavaScript is the backbone of most web applications, powering everything from dynamic user interfaces to real-time interactions. Below are some real-world examples of how JavaScript is used in modern web apps:

- **Interactive Forms**: JavaScript is widely used to validate forms in real-time, providing instant feedback to users. For example, in a registration form, JavaScript can ensure that the user's password meets certain requirements (like length or complexity) before submission.

javascript

```
const            passwordInput            =
document.querySelector('#password');
passwordInput.addEventListener('input',
function() {
    if (passwordInput.value.length < 8) {

passwordInput.setCustomValidity("Password
must be at least 8 characters long.");
    } else {

passwordInput.setCustomValidity("");
    }
});
```

- **Dynamic Content Updates**: JavaScript enables the dynamic updating of content on the web page without requiring a full page reload. This is achieved through techniques like AJAX (Asynchronous JavaScript and XML). For instance, JavaScript can be used to fetch new data from the server and update the page in real-time.

31

```javascript
javascript

function loadNewContent() {

fetch('https://api.example.com/posts')
        .then(response => response.json())
        .then(posts => {
            let         contentDiv        =
document.querySelector('#content');
            posts.forEach(post => {
                let         postDiv        =
document.createElement('div');
                postDiv.textContent        =
post.title;

contentDiv.appendChild(postDiv);
            });
        });
}
```

- **Interactive Maps**: JavaScript is also used in web applications that require interactive maps, such as ride-sharing apps or real estate websites. Libraries like Leaflet and Google Maps API allow developers to display and interact with maps on their websites.

```javascript
javascript
```

```
const          map          =          new
google.maps.Map(document.getElementById('
map'), {
    center: { lat: 40.7128, lng: -74.0060
}, // New York City coordinates
    zoom: 10
});
```

These examples show how JavaScript powers dynamic functionality, making web apps more engaging, interactive, and user-friendly.

This chapter has covered essential JavaScript fundamentals, including core concepts like variables, functions, and arrays, as well as advanced features such as arrow functions, promises, and async/await. Understanding the DOM and event handling is crucial for any web developer, as these allow interaction with the HTML content. The real-world examples highlight how JavaScript is used in everyday web applications. In the next chapter, we'll delve into the specifics of setting up and using React, one of the most popular JavaScript frameworks for building modern web apps.

CHAPTER 3

INTRODUCTION TO REACT: GETTING STARTED

What is React and Why is it Popular?

React is a powerful JavaScript library developed by Facebook (now Meta) for building user interfaces, specifically single-page applications (SPAs). React allows developers to create large web applications that can update and render efficiently in response to data changes, making it ideal for building dynamic, data-driven user interfaces.

React's popularity stems from its simplicity, flexibility, and performance. Here's why React has become one of the most widely used front-end libraries:

- **Component-Based Architecture**: React uses a component-based approach, where the UI is divided into reusable, self-contained components. Each component has its own state and logic, making it easier to manage and scale the application.
- **Virtual DOM**: One of React's standout features is its virtual DOM. The virtual DOM is a lightweight of the

actual DOM. When a component's state changes, React first updates the virtual DOM and compares it with the previous version. It then calculates the most efficient way to update the real DOM, leading to faster rendering and better performance.

- **Declarative Syntax**: React uses a declarative syntax, meaning that developers describe *what* the UI should look like based on the state of the application, rather than *how* to update the UI. This makes React code easier to understand and debug.

- **Large Ecosystem**: React has a large ecosystem of tools, libraries, and community resources. From state management libraries like Redux to component libraries like Material-UI, the ecosystem makes it easy to integrate additional functionality into your app.

- **Cross-Platform Development**: React is not limited to web applications. With React Native, developers can also build mobile apps for iOS and Android using the same React principles.

Setting Up React with Create React App

Setting up React in your development environment can be done in a few easy steps, thanks to Create React App, a tool that sets up

35

everything you need to start building React applications with minimal configuration. Here's how to get started:

1. **Install Node.js**: React requires Node.js to run. You can download the latest version of Node.js from https://nodejs.org. This will also install npm (Node Package Manager), which is used to manage dependencies.

2. **Create a React App**: Open your terminal and run the following command to create a new React application using Create React App:

```bash
```

```bash
npx create-react-app my-app
```

This command creates a new directory called `my-app` with all the necessary files and configurations.

3. **Navigate to Your App Directory**: Once the setup is complete, navigate into your project folder:

```bash
```

```bash
cd my-app
```

4. **Start the Development Server**: Run the following command to start the development server and open the app in your browser:

```
bash
```

```
npm start
```

This will open the default browser with the React app running at `http://localhost:3000`. By default, you'll see the "React logo" and some boilerplate text. You can now start modifying the code.

5. **Project Structure**: The `create-react-app` tool generates a project structure with key files and folders:
    - **public/**: Contains the static assets, like `index.html`, which is the template for the React app.
    - **src/**: Contains the JavaScript files that make up the app, including `App.js`, where most of your React code will reside.

JSX and Virtual DOM Explained

- **JSX (JavaScript XML)**: React uses JSX, which allows you to write HTML-like syntax directly within JavaScript. This makes it easier to define the structure and layout of components. Even though it looks similar to HTML, JSX is compiled into regular JavaScript code. For example:

37

```jsx
jsx
```

```jsx
const element = <h1>Hello, World!</h1>;
```

JSX allows you to integrate JavaScript expressions directly into the markup using curly braces {}. For example, to display dynamic content:

```jsx
jsx
```

```jsx
const name = 'John';
const element = <h1>Hello, {name}!</h1>;
```

JSX is not mandatory in React, but it is highly recommended for building user interfaces because it makes the code more readable and concise.

- **Virtual DOM**: The virtual DOM is a key feature of React that improves performance. When a component's state or props change, React doesn't immediately update the real DOM. Instead, it creates a virtual DOM, which is a lightweight of the actual DOM. React then compares the current virtual DOM with the previous one, and calculates the minimum number of changes required to update the real DOM. This process is known as "reconciliation."

The virtual DOM helps optimize rendering performance by reducing unnecessary updates to the real DOM, which is slow and resource-intensive. This makes React highly efficient when building dynamic user interfaces.

Building a Simple React App: "Hello World" Example

Now that you have a basic understanding of React, let's build a simple "Hello World" application to demonstrate how React works in practice.

1. **Create a New Component**: In your `src` folder, open the `App.js` file. Replace the default code with the following:

```jsx
import React from 'react';

function App() {
    const name = 'World';
    return <h1>Hello, {name}!</h1>;
}

export default App;
```

This component is a function that returns JSX. The `name` variable holds the value `World`, and it is injected into the JSX using curly braces.

39

2. **Add More Interactivity**: Let's add a button that updates the name when clicked. We will introduce React's **useState** hook to manage state in a functional component:

```jsx
import React, { useState } from 'react';

function App() {
    const      [name,      setName]      =
useState('World');

    const handleClick = () => {
        setName('React');
    };

    return (
        <div>
            <h1>Hello, {name}!</h1>
            <button
onClick={handleClick}>Change Name</button>
        </div>
    );
}

export default App;
```

In this example, we use `useState` to create a `name` state variable and a `setName` function to update its value. The

40

`handleClick` function updates the name when the button is clicked, and React re-renders the component with the new value.

3. **Start the App**: Save your changes and go back to your terminal. Run `npm start` to see the app in action. You should see the greeting "Hello, World!" and a button. When you click the button, the text should change to "Hello, React!"

In this chapter, we've covered the basics of React, including its popularity, how to set up a React app using Create React App, and the fundamentals of JSX and the virtual DOM. We also built a simple "Hello World" React app with interactive functionality. In the next chapter, we'll dive deeper into React components and explore how to build more complex UIs using functional components, props, and state.

CHAPTER 4

UNDERSTANDING COMPONENTS IN REACT

What Are Components and Why Are They Essential in React?

In React, **components** are the fundamental building blocks of a web application. A component in React is essentially a JavaScript function or class that accepts inputs (called **props**) and returns a React element that describes what should appear on the screen. Components enable developers to break down complex user interfaces into smaller, reusable, and manageable pieces. This modularity is one of the key reasons why React is so popular.

The primary purpose of components is to create a clean separation of concerns, allowing you to build and maintain UIs more efficiently. Each component can handle its own state, logic, and rendering, which makes it easier to manage and scale the application.

In a React application, you might have components for various parts of the interface, such as headers, buttons, forms, and even entire sections of the page. Components can be composed together, meaning one component can contain other components, forming a component tree that describes the full UI.

Functional vs Class Components

React supports two types of components: **functional components** and **class components**. Both types serve the same purpose of defining a part of the UI, but they differ in syntax and how they handle state and lifecycle methods.

- **Functional Components**: Functional components are the simpler of the two. They are just JavaScript functions that return JSX. In earlier versions of React, functional components were stateless, but with the introduction of **Hooks** in React 16.8, functional components can now manage state and side effects.

   Syntax: A functional component is simply a JavaScript function that returns JSX.

```javascript
function Greeting() {
    return <h1>Hello, React!</h1>;
}
```

43

In this example, `Greeting` is a stateless functional component that simply renders a greeting message.

Using State with Hooks: Functional components can now use the `useState` hook to manage internal state.

```javascript
import React, { useState } from 'react';

function Counter() {
    const [count, setCount] = useState(0);

    const increment = () => setCount(count + 1);

    return (
        <div>
            <h1>{count}</h1>
            <button onClick={increment}>Increment</button>
        </div>
    );
}
```

- **Class Components**: Class components are ES6 classes that extend `React.Component`. They are more complex than functional components and can manage state and lifecycle methods directly. However, with the introduction of hooks, functional components have become more popular due to their simpler syntax and less boilerplate code.

Syntax: A class component requires a constructor and the render() method that returns JSX.

```javascript

class Greeting extends React.Component {
    render() {
        return <h1>Hello, React from a
class component!</h1>;
    }
}
```

State and Lifecycle Methods: Class components can manage state using this.state and modify it with this.setState(). They also provide lifecycle methods, such as componentDidMount() and componentDidUpdate(), which allow you to perform side effects at different points in a component's life.

```javascript

class Counter extends React.Component {
    constructor(props) {
        super(props);
        this.state = { count: 0 };
```

45

```
        }

    increment = () => {
        this.setState({              count:
    this.state.count + 1 });
        };

    render() {
        return (
            <div>

<h1>{this.state.count}</h1>
                    <button
onClick={this.increment}>Increment</butto
n>
            </div>
        );
        }
    }
```

Conclusion: While class components are still supported and widely used in many existing codebases, functional components with hooks are now the preferred choice in modern React development due to their simplicity and flexibility.

Props and State: Data Flow in React Apps

One of the most important concepts in React is the flow of data between components, which is handled using **props** and **state**.

- **Props** (short for properties) are read-only data passed from a parent component to a child component. Props allow data to flow down the component tree, ensuring that child components can receive and use the data provided by their parent components.

  Example of Props:

  ```javascript
  function Welcome(props) {
      return <h1>Hello, {props.name}!</h1>;
  }

  function App() {
      return <Welcome name="Alice" />;
  }
  ```

  In this example, Welcome is a functional component that receives the name prop and displays it in an h1 element. The App component is the parent component, passing the value "Alice" as the name prop to the Welcome component.

  Props are immutable in the child component, meaning the child cannot change the props it receives. If the data needs to be changed, it must be done in the parent component and passed down again.

- **State** represents data that changes over time and is specific to a component. State is managed inside the component itself and can be modified using the `setState()` method (for class components) or the `useState()` hook (for functional components). Unlike props, state is mutable and can be updated as a result of user interactions, API calls, or other events.

Example of State in Functional Components:

```javascript
import React, { useState } from 'react';

function Counter() {
    const [count, setCount] = useState(0);

    const increment = () => setCount(count + 1);

    return (
        <div>
            <h1>{count}</h1>
            <button onClick={increment}>Increment</button>
        </div>
```

```
    );
}
```

In this example, the `Counter` component has a state variable called `count`, initialized to 0. When the button is clicked, the `increment` function updates the state by increasing the count, triggering a re-render of the component with the new count.

Data Flow: In React, data flows in a unidirectional manner:

1. The parent component passes data down to child components through **props**.
2. Child components cannot modify their props; they can only use the data passed to them.
3. If a child component needs to modify its data, it can use **state**.
4. Changes in state trigger re-renders of the component, updating the UI.

Real-World Example: Building a Reusable Component

Let's build a reusable button component that can be used in different parts of your application, with different labels and click behaviors.

1. **Create the Button Component**: In the `src` folder, create a new file `Button.js` and define the component:

```javascript
import React from 'react';

function Button({ label, onClick }) {
    return (
        <button onClick={onClick}>
            {label}
        </button>
    );
}

export default Button;
```

Here, the `Button` component accepts two props: `label` (the text to be displayed on the button) and `onClick` (the function to be executed when the button is clicked).

2. **Use the Button Component**: Now, in `App.js`, we will import and use the `Button` component, passing different props to customize it:

```javascript
import React, { useState } from 'react';
import Button from './Button';
```

50

```
function App() {
    const [count, setCount] = useState(0);

    const increment = () => setCount(count
+ 1);
    const decrement = () => setCount(count
- 1);

    return (
        <div>
            <h1>Count: {count}</h1>
            <Button    label="Increment"
onClick={increment} />
            <Button    label="Decrement"
onClick={decrement} />
        </div>
    );
}

export default App;
```

In this example, the `Button` component is used twice, once for the "Increment" button and once for the "Decrement" button. Both buttons reuse the same `Button` component, but each has different behavior because we pass different `onClick` functions.

In this chapter, we have covered the core concepts of React components, including the differences between functional and class components, how props and state facilitate data flow in React apps, and how to create reusable components. As you continue building more complex applications, understanding components will be crucial to managing the structure and behavior of your UI. In the next chapter, we'll explore React's lifecycle methods and hooks, which allow you to handle side effects and manage state more effectively.

CHAPTER 5

REACT LIFECYCLE METHODS AND HOOKS

Understanding React Lifecycle Methods (componentDidMount, componentWillUnmount)

React components have a lifecycle that consists of different phases: mounting, updating, and unmounting. During these phases, React provides several lifecycle methods that give you control over what happens at different points in the component's life.

Lifecycle methods are used primarily in **class components** to handle tasks like fetching data, updating the UI, or cleaning up resources when the component is no longer needed.

Here are two of the most important lifecycle methods:

- **componentDidMount**: This method is called once after the component has been rendered to the screen. It's typically used for tasks that require interaction with external APIs, such as fetching data or subscribing to a service.

```javascript

class MyComponent extends React.Component
{
    componentDidMount() {
        console.log('Component          has
mounted');
        // Fetch  data  or  perform  side-
effects here
    }

    render() {
        return <div>Hello, World!</div>;
    }
}
```

In this example, componentDidMount() is used to log a message to the console once the component is mounted.

- **componentWillUnmount**: This method is called just before a component is removed from the DOM. It's useful for cleaning up resources like cancelling API requests, unsubscribing from services, or clearing timers to prevent memory leaks.

```javascript

class MyComponent extends React.Component
{
```

```
componentWillUnmount() {
    console.log('Component is about to
be unmounted');
    // Clean up resources here
}

render() {
    return <div>Goodbye, World!</div>;
}
}
```

`componentWillUnmount()` is important for cleanup tasks, ensuring that no unnecessary operations continue when the component is no longer needed.

Introduction to Hooks: useState, useEffect, useContext

With the introduction of **React Hooks** in React 16.8, functional components can now have the same capabilities as class components, including managing state and handling side effects. Hooks simplify the code, making it more readable and reducing the need for boilerplate.

Here are the most commonly used hooks in modern React development:

- **useState**: The `useState` hook allows you to add state to functional components. It returns an array with two elements: the current state value and a function to update that state.

```javascript
import React, { useState } from 'react';

function Counter() {
    const [count, setCount] = useState(0);

    const increment = () => setCount(count + 1);

    return (
        <div>
            <h1>{count}</h1>
            <button
onClick={increment}>Increment</button>
        </div>
    );
}
```

In this example, `useState(0)` initializes the `count` state to 0, and `setCount` is the function used to update it when the button is clicked.

- **useEffect**: The `useEffect` hook allows you to perform side effects in functional components, such as fetching data, updating the DOM, or subscribing to a service. It is similar to lifecycle methods like `componentDidMount`, `componentDidUpdate`, and `componentWillUnmount` in class components.

```javascript

import React, { useState, useEffect } from 'react';

function FetchData() {
    const    [data,    setData]    =
useState(null);

    useEffect(() => {

fetch('https://api.example.com/data')
            .then(response            =>
response.json())
            .then(data => setData(data));
    }, []); // Empty dependency array
ensures this runs only once, similar to
componentDidMount

    if (!data) {
        return <p>Loading...</p>;
    }
```

```
return
<div>{JSON.stringify(data)}</div>;
}
```

In this example, `useEffect` is used to fetch data from an API after the component mounts. The empty dependency array `[]` ensures that the effect runs only once, similar to `componentDidMount`.

- **useContext**: The `useContext` hook allows you to access the value of a context directly in a functional component. It simplifies passing data through the component tree without having to pass props down manually at every level.

```javascript
import React, { useState, useContext, createContext } from 'react';

const ThemeContext = createContext();

function ThemedComponent() {
    const theme = useContext(ThemeContext);
    return <div style={{ background: theme === 'dark' ? 'black' : 'white' }}>Themed Component</div>;
```

```
}

function App() {
    const     [theme,     setTheme]     =
    useState('light');

    return (
        <ThemeContext.Provider
    value={theme}>
            <button     onClick={()     =>
    setTheme(theme  ===  'light'  ?  'dark'  :
    'light')}>Toggle Theme</button>
            <ThemedComponent />
        </ThemeContext.Provider>
    );
}
```

Here, `useContext` provides access to the current theme value in `ThemedComponent`, which was provided by `ThemeContext.Provider` in the parent component `App`. This avoids the need for prop drilling (passing props through multiple layers of components).

When to Use Lifecycle Methods vs Hooks

Lifecycle methods are specific to **class components**, whereas **hooks** are used in **functional components**. React encourages the use of functional components with hooks for a simpler and more concise syntax.

- **Use lifecycle methods in class components**: If you're working with class components, you'll need to use lifecycle methods to handle operations like mounting, updating, and unmounting. For example, if you need to fetch data after the component mounts or clean up resources before unmounting, you would use `componentDidMount` and `componentWillUnmount`.

- **Use hooks in functional components**: In modern React development, it's highly recommended to use functional components with hooks. Hooks like `useState`, `useEffect`, and `useContext` give you all the capabilities of class components while providing a cleaner and more readable syntax.

For example, if you're handling side effects like fetching data, managing subscriptions, or interacting with the DOM, you can use `useEffect` in a functional component. If you need to manage state, you can use `useState`. The flexibility of hooks allows for better code reuse and less boilerplate.

Real-World Example: Using Hooks for State Management in a Dynamic App

Let's look at a more complex example of a dynamic app using hooks for state management. We'll build a simple to-do list where users can add, remove, and mark tasks as completed.

1. **App Setup**: We'll create the `TodoApp` component using `useState` to manage the state of tasks and `useEffect` to load tasks from local storage when the app loads.

```javascript
import React, { useState, useEffect } from 'react';

function TodoApp() {
    const [tasks, setTasks] = useState([]);
    const [newTask, setNewTask] = useState("");

    useEffect(() => {
        // Load tasks from local storage on component mount
        const savedTasks = JSON.parse(localStorage.getItem("tasks")) || [];
        setTasks(savedTasks);
    }, []); // Only run once when the component mounts
```

61

```
useEffect(() => {
    // Save tasks to local storage when
tasks change
    localStorage.setItem("tasks",
JSON.stringify(tasks));
}, [tasks]); // Run whenever tasks
change

const addTask = () => {
    if (newTask) {
        const    updatedTasks    =
[...tasks, { text: newTask, completed:
false }];
        setTasks(updatedTasks);
        setNewTask(""); // Clear the
input field
    }
};

const toggleTask = (index) => {
    const    updatedTasks    =
tasks.map((task, i) =>
        i === index ? { ...task,
completed: !task.completed } : task
    );
    setTasks(updatedTasks);
};

const deleteTask = (index) => {
```

```
        const         updatedTasks        =
tasks.filter((_, i) => i !== index);
        setTasks(updatedTasks);
    };

    return (
        <div>
            <h1>Todo List</h1>
            <input
                type="text"
                value={newTask}
                onChange={(e)             =>
setNewTask(e.target.value)}
                placeholder="New task"
            />
            <button  onClick={addTask}>Add
Task</button>
            <ul>
                {tasks.map((task,    index)
=> (
                    <li key={index}>
                        <span
                            style={{

textDecoration:  task.completed  ?  "line-
through" : "none"
                            }}
                            onClick={()  =>
toggleTask(index)}
```

```
                              >
                                {task.text}
                              </span>
                              <button
onClick={()                                    =>
deleteTask(index)}>Delete</button>
                          </li>
                    ))}
                </ul>
            </div>
        );
}


export default TodoApp;
```

- o **State Management**: `useState` is used to manage the state of the tasks (`tasks`) and the input field (`newTask`).
- o **Side Effects**: `useEffect` is used to load tasks from local storage when the app mounts and to save tasks to local storage whenever the tasks list changes.
- o **Dynamic Updates**: Users can add tasks, toggle them as completed, and delete tasks, all of which trigger updates to the state and the UI.

In this chapter, we covered React's lifecycle methods and hooks, explaining their differences and how to use them effectively in class and functional components. We also explored how to manage state and side effects in functional components with `useState` and `useEffect`, and provided a real-world example of a dynamic app to illustrate the concepts. In the next chapter, we will dive deeper into handling forms in React, a common task for many web applications.

CHAPTER 6

STATE MANAGEMENT IN REACT WITH REDUX

What is Redux and Why Do We Need It?

Managing state in a React application can become complex as the application grows. In small applications, state management with `useState` or `useReducer` might be sufficient. However, as the app scales and data needs to be shared across multiple components, maintaining state consistency can become difficult. This is where **Redux** comes in.

Redux is a state management library that helps manage application state in a predictable way, making it easier to handle state changes and share state across the entire application. Redux is often used in React applications, but it can be integrated with other libraries as well.

The core idea behind Redux is that the entire state of the application is stored in a single JavaScript object called the **store**. This central store can be accessed by any component, and when components need to update the state, they dispatch **actions** that are processed by **reducers**. This predictable flow makes it easier to manage and debug large-scale applications.

Why We Need Redux:

- **Predictable State**: Redux provides a predictable way to manage state with clear rules about how state is updated. The state is immutable, meaning it cannot be modified directly, ensuring that state updates are always predictable and traceable.

- **Centralized State**: Instead of passing props down multiple layers or using local state in every component, Redux allows you to store your application's state in a central location, making it accessible from any component in your app.

- **Easier Debugging and Testing**: Redux makes it easier to debug and test because you can trace every action and state change. You can log all actions and states, and even replay them to reproduce bugs.

Setting Up Redux in a React App

To use Redux with React, we need to install Redux and React-Redux (the official Redux bindings for React). Follow these steps to set it up:

1. **Install Redux and React-Redux**: Open your terminal and run the following command in the project directory:

```bash
bash
```

```
npm install redux react-redux
```

2. **Create the Redux Store**: The store is the central place where your application state is stored. You need to create a Redux store and define how the state will change using reducers.

   Create a file store.js:

```javascript
javascript
```

```javascript
import { createStore } from 'redux';

// Initial state of the app
const initialState = {
    count: 0,
};

// Reducer function to update the state
const counterReducer = (state = initialState, action) => {
    switch (action.type) {
        case 'INCREMENT':
```

```
                    return    {   ...state,   count:
state.count + 1 };
        case 'DECREMENT':
                    return    {   ...state,   count:
state.count - 1 };
        default:
            return state;
    }
};

// Create Redux store
const store = createStore(counterReducer);

export default store;
```

In this example, the `counterReducer` defines how the state should change based on the action. The initial state contains a `count` property, and the reducer updates this count when an `INCREMENT` or `DECREMENT` action is dispatched.

3. **Provide the Redux Store to React**: To connect Redux with React, you need to wrap your application in a `<Provider>` component, which makes the Redux store available to all components in the application.

Modify the `index.js` (or `App.js`) file to include the `Provider`:

69

```javascript

import React from 'react';
import ReactDOM from 'react-dom';
import { Provider } from 'react-redux';
import App from './App';
import store from './store'; // Import the
Redux store

ReactDOM.render(
    <Provider store={store}>
        <App />
    </Provider>,
    document.getElementById('root')
);
```

By wrapping your app with the `Provider`, you ensure that the Redux store is available to all components within your app.

Actions, Reducers, and the Store: Understanding the Flow of Data

- **Actions**: Actions are plain JavaScript objects that describe what happened in the application. Actions must have a `type` property, and they may also have a `payload` with additional data. Actions are dispatched from components to trigger state updates.

```javascript
const incrementAction = { type: 'INCREMENT'
};
const decrementAction = { type: 'DECREMENT'
};
```

- **Reducers**: Reducers are pure functions that determine how the state changes in response to an action. A reducer takes the current state and an action, and returns the new state.

In the previous `counterReducer` example, the reducer handles two actions: INCREMENT and DECREMENT. Each time an action is dispatched, the reducer determines how the state should change based on the action type.

```javascript
const    counterReducer    =    (state    =
initialState, action) => {
    switch (action.type) {
        case 'INCREMENT':
            return {  ...state,  count:
state.count + 1 };
        case 'DECREMENT':
```

71

```
            return    {   ...state,   count:
state.count - 1 };
        default:
            return state;
    }
};
```

- **The Store**: The store is a JavaScript object that holds the application state. It provides methods to access the state, dispatch actions, and subscribe to state changes.

```javascript
const store = createStore(counterReducer);
store.dispatch(incrementAction);          //
Dispatch an action to update the state
console.log(store.getState()); // Get the
updated state
```

Real-World Example: Building a Shopping Cart with Redux

Let's build a real-world example using Redux: a shopping cart where users can add items, remove items, and view the cart contents.

1. **Create Action Types**: First, define action types for adding and removing items from the cart.

```
javascript
```

```javascript
const ADD_ITEM = 'ADD_ITEM';
const REMOVE_ITEM = 'REMOVE_ITEM';
```

2. **Create Actions**: Define action creators for adding and removing items.

```
javascript
```

```javascript
const addItem = (item) => {
    return {
        type: ADD_ITEM,
        payload: item,
    };
};

const removeItem = (itemId) => {
    return {
        type: REMOVE_ITEM,
        payload: itemId,
    };
};
```

3. **Create Reducer**: The reducer will manage the state of the cart. It will handle actions to add or remove items.

```
javascript
```

```javascript
const initialState = {
```

```javascript
    cart: [],
};

const cartReducer = (state = initialState,
action) => {
    switch (action.type) {
        case ADD_ITEM:
            return {  ...state,  cart:
[...state.cart, action.payload] };
        case REMOVE_ITEM:
            return {
                ...state,
                cart:
state.cart.filter((item)  =>  item.id  !==
action.payload),
            };
        default:
            return state;
    }
};
```

4. **Create Redux Store**: Create the store using the
   cartReducer.

```javascript
javascript

const store = createStore(cartReducer);
```

74

5. **Connect Redux to React Components**: Use `useSelector` to access the state and `useDispatch` to dispatch actions in the `Cart` component.

```javascript
import React from 'react';
import { useDispatch, useSelector } from
'react-redux';
import { addItem, removeItem } from
'./actions';

function Cart() {
    const cart = useSelector((state) =>
state.cart);
    const dispatch = useDispatch();

    const handleAddItem = () => {
        const newItem = { id: Date.now(),
name: 'New Item', price: 20 };
        dispatch(addItem(newItem));
    };

    const handleRemoveItem = (itemId) => {
        dispatch(removeItem(itemId));
    };

    return (
        <div>
```

75

```
<h2>Shopping Cart</h2>
<button
onClick={handleAddItem}>Add Item</button>
<ul>
    {cart.map((item) => (
        <li key={item.id}>
            {item.name}            -
${item.price}{' '}
            <button
onClick={()                      =>
handleRemoveItem(item.id)}>Remove</button
>
            </li>
    ))}
</ul>
</div>
);
}

export default Cart;
```

In this example, the `Cart` component displays a list of items in the shopping cart. The `addItem` and `removeItem` actions are dispatched to update the Redux store when items are added or removed.

6. **Wrap the App with `Provider`**: Finally, wrap the app with the `Provider` to connect Redux to your React app.

```javascript

import React from 'react';
import ReactDOM from 'react-dom';
import { Provider } from 'react-redux';
import App from './App';
import store from './store';

ReactDOM.render(
    <Provider store={store}>
        <App />
    </Provider>,
    document.getElementById('root')
);
```

In this chapter, we introduced Redux as a state management tool, explained how to set it up in a React app, and described how actions, reducers, and the store work together to manage state. We also built a real-world example—a shopping cart—using Redux to handle adding and removing items. Redux can be incredibly helpful in large-scale applications where state needs to be shared across many components. In the next chapter, we will explore advanced React concepts like routing and managing forms.

CHAPTER 7

ADVANCED REACT: CODE SPLITTING AND LAZY LOADING

Understanding the Importance of Code Splitting

As your React applications grow larger and more complex, the size of your JavaScript bundle increases as well. A large bundle can slow down the initial loading time of your app, negatively affecting the user experience. This is where **code splitting** comes into play.

Code splitting is the technique of splitting your JavaScript bundle into smaller, more manageable chunks. Instead of loading the entire application at once, only the necessary parts of the application are loaded when needed. This can greatly improve the performance of your app by reducing the initial loading time and speeding up the application's response time.

There are two key reasons why code splitting is important:

- **Faster Initial Load**: With code splitting, only the code required for the initial view is loaded first. Other parts of the application (such as routes or components that aren't immediately necessary) are loaded later, as the user interacts with the app.

- **Reduced Bundle Size**: By breaking up your app into smaller pieces, you can reduce the overall size of the initial bundle, making the app faster to load and more efficient to run.

React offers several tools and methods to achieve code splitting, and one of the most effective approaches is **lazy loading**.

Implementing Lazy Loading with React.lazy and Suspense

React provides built-in support for lazy loading components using the `React.lazy()` function and `Suspense` component. The `React.lazy()` function allows you to dynamically import a component only when it is needed, which helps with code splitting. The `Suspense` component lets you define a fallback UI (such as a loading spinner) while waiting for the component to load.

Here's how you can implement lazy loading in React:

1. **Using `React.lazy()`**: The `React.lazy()` function takes a function that dynamically imports a component using `import()`. This will only load the component when it is rendered for the first time.

```javascript
import React, { Suspense } from 'react';

// Lazy load the component
const About = React.lazy(() =>
import('./About'));

function App() {
    return (
        <div>
            <h1>Welcome to My App</h1>
            {/* Suspense provides a
fallback while the component is loading */}
            <Suspense
fallback={<div>Loading...</div>}>
                <About />
            </Suspense>
        </div>
    );
}

export default App;
```

In this example:

- o The `About` component is loaded lazily using `React.lazy()` when the `App` component is rendered.

o The `Suspense` component is used to wrap the lazy-loaded `About` component and display a loading message (`<div>Loading...</div>`) while the component is being fetched.

2. **Why Use `Suspense`?**: The `Suspense` component is a React feature that allows you to control what to render while your lazy-loaded component is being fetched. Without `Suspense`, lazy-loaded components would return a promise, which can't be rendered. `Suspense` solves this problem by rendering a fallback UI (e.g., a loading spinner or text) while the component is loading.

3. **Dynamic Import of Other Resources**: You can also use `React.lazy()` for other types of dynamic imports, such as images or other non-component resources. This can further optimize the loading process by ensuring that only essential resources are loaded initially.

Real-World Example: Optimizing App Performance with Dynamic Imports

Let's look at a real-world example where we use code splitting and lazy loading to optimize the performance of an app. In this case, we will create a simple e-commerce app that lazily loads different product pages and only fetches the necessary components when needed.

81

1. **Create Product Components**: We have multiple product components, such as `ProductList`, `ProductDetails`, and `Checkout`. Instead of loading all of them at once, we will lazy-load the product pages as the user navigates through the app.

   javascript

   ```javascript
   // Lazy load ProductList component
   const ProductList = React.lazy(() =>
   import('./ProductList'));

   // Lazy load ProductDetails component
   const ProductDetails = React.lazy(() =>
   import('./ProductDetails'));

   // Lazy load Checkout component
   const Checkout = React.lazy(() =>
   import('./Checkout'));
   ```

2. **App Component with Routes**: In the `App` component, we will set up a basic route system where different components are displayed depending on the user's interaction. We will use React Router to navigate between pages.

   javascript

   ```javascript
   import React, { Suspense } from 'react';
   ```

```
import { BrowserRouter as Router, Route,
Switch } from 'react-router-dom';

function App() {
    return (
        <Router>
            <div>
                <h1>My E-Commerce App</h1>
                <Suspense
fallback={<div>Loading...</div>}>
                    <Switch>
                        <Route
path="/products"   component={ProductList}
/>
                        <Route
path="/product/:id"
component={ProductDetails} />
                        <Route
path="/checkout" component={Checkout} />
                    </Switch>
                </Suspense>
            </div>
        </Router>
    );
}

export default App;
```

- o We use `React.lazy()` to lazily load each component: `ProductList`, `ProductDetails`, and `Checkout`.
- o The `Suspense` component wraps the entire route section to handle the loading state of these components.
- o The `Switch` component from `react-router-dom` is used to navigate between different routes in the app.

3. **Why Lazy Load Routes?**:
   - o **Initial Load Optimization**: Instead of loading all product details and checkout pages immediately, only the `ProductList` component is loaded initially, improving the app's first render time.
   - o **Improved User Experience**: By loading each component dynamically as needed, the app is more responsive. Users don't have to wait for unnecessary data to be fetched upfront. Components like `ProductDetails` or `Checkout` are only loaded when the user navigates to them.
   - o **Reduced Bundle Size**: Code splitting ensures that each bundle is smaller and more efficient. Only the code required for the current route is fetched, reducing the amount of JavaScript sent to the browser.

4. **Fallback UI During Loading**:

    o   In this example, the `Suspense` component shows a "Loading..." message while each page (product list, product details, or checkout) is being fetched. You can customize this fallback to display a loading spinner or skeleton screen, enhancing the user experience.

```javascript

<Suspense fallback={<div>Loading... Please
wait</div>}>
    {/* Lazy-loaded components */}
</Suspense>
```

This can be further customized for each component to provide more context-specific loading states.

Additional Optimizations with Dynamic Imports

Apart from lazy loading React components, you can also apply dynamic imports to other parts of your app to further optimize performance:

*   **Images**: If your app has large images that are not initially visible, you can dynamically import them when needed (e.g., when they enter the viewport). This can be achieved

with `React.lazy()` and `Suspense` for images or libraries like `react-lazyload` for lazy loading images.

- **Third-Party Libraries**: Libraries like charting libraries, UI component libraries, or video players can be imported dynamically only when required. This reduces the size of the initial bundle and ensures that the user only loads necessary code.

In this chapter, we've covered the importance of **code splitting** and **lazy loading** in React to improve app performance. We learned how to use `React.lazy()` and `Suspense` to implement lazy loading, and we built a real-world example of an e-commerce app where components are loaded dynamically based on user interaction. By optimizing the loading process, we ensure a faster, more efficient user experience. In the next chapter, we will explore React Router and how to manage navigation within a React application effectively.

CHAPTER 8

INTRODUCTION TO ANGULAR: GETTING STARTED

What is Angular and How Does It Differ from React?

Angular is a **full-fledged framework** for building dynamic web applications, created and maintained by Google. Unlike **React**, which is a **JavaScript library** focused solely on building user interfaces (UI), Angular provides a complete solution for building web apps. It includes built-in tools for routing, forms management, HTTP requests, and more. React, on the other hand, is more flexible and leaves more decisions to the developer regarding how to structure the app, while Angular provides a more opinionated and comprehensive approach to app development.

Here's a comparison between **Angular** and **React**:

1. **Framework vs. Library**:
   o **Angular**: A complete framework that offers a structured way to build apps with built-in tools for routing, state management, forms, and HTTP requests.

87

- o **React**: A JavaScript library focused primarily on building UI components. It's lighter and requires additional tools (like React Router for routing or Redux for state management) for full-featured app development.

2. **Data Binding**:
   - o **Angular**: Supports two-way data binding, meaning changes in the UI automatically update the application state and vice versa. This is achieved using Angular's declarative syntax and binding expressions.
   - o **React**: Uses one-way data flow, where data is passed from parent components to child components through props. For two-way binding, React uses a state management pattern, typically via `useState` and event handlers.

3. **Component Structure**:
   - o **Angular**: Uses a class-based component structure with decorators (e.g., `@Component`) that provide metadata for the component. Angular components are usually larger and more feature-rich due to the framework's built-in services and dependency injection.
   - o **React**: Typically uses a function-based component structure (with hooks) or class components, allowing developers to define the UI

88

structure and logic separately. React's component structure is simpler but requires more setup when additional features are needed.

4. **Learning Curve**:

   o **Angular**: Angular has a steeper learning curve due to its comprehensive nature. It comes with a lot of built-in tools and concepts (like modules, services, directives, and dependency injection), which can be overwhelming for beginners.

   o **React**: React has a gentler learning curve since it focuses mainly on building UIs. However, as the app grows, developers will need to add libraries for routing, state management, and other features.

5. **Tooling**:

   o **Angular**: Comes with the **Angular CLI** (Command Line Interface) that automates common tasks such as project setup, development, testing, and deployment.

   o **React**: React can be set up using Create React App or custom configurations, but the ecosystem is less opinionated than Angular's, requiring additional tools for specific tasks.

When to Choose Angular?

- You need a complete solution for building large-scale applications with built-in features (like routing, forms, HTTP handling).
- You prefer a more opinionated framework that provides a structured way of building apps.
- Your team is comfortable with TypeScript (Angular is built with TypeScript, which provides type safety and better tooling support).

When to Choose React?

- You want more flexibility in your development approach.
- You are building a simple-to-medium-sized application and don't need a lot of built-in features.
- You prefer a library that works well with JavaScript and can easily integrate with other libraries.

Setting Up Angular with Angular CLI

The **Angular CLI** (Command Line Interface) is a powerful tool that helps developers set up, build, test, and deploy Angular applications. It simplifies many tasks by automating them, such as generating components, services, and modules, as well as running tests and building the production-ready app.

Here's how to get started with Angular using Angular CLI:

1. **Install Angular CLI**: First, you need to install Angular CLI globally on your machine. Open your terminal and run:

```bash
npm install -g @angular/cli
```

2. **Create a New Angular Project**: Once Angular CLI is installed, you can create a new Angular project by running:

```bash
ng new my-angular-app
```

This command will prompt you with a few configuration options, such as whether to include routing and which stylesheet format to use. For a basic app, you can go with the default options.

3. **Navigate to the Project Directory**:

```bash
cd my-angular-app
```

4. **Serve the Application**: To start the development server and see your app in action, run:

```bash

ng serve
```

This will start the development server and your app will be available at `http://localhost:4200/`. You can make changes to your app and see the updates in real-time.

Components and Templates in Angular

In Angular, **components** are the fundamental building blocks of an application. A component in Angular consists of:

- **A TypeScript class** that defines the logic of the component.
- **An HTML template** that defines the view or structure of the UI.
- **CSS styles** that define the appearance of the component.

Here's how Angular components are structured:

1. **Creating a Component**: You can generate a new component using the Angular CLI. For example, to create a `Header` component, run:

```bash
ng generate component header
```

This will create a new `header` component with the following files:

- o `header.component.ts` (TypeScript logic)
- o `header.component.html` (HTML template)
- o `header.component.css` (CSS styles)
- o `header.component.spec.ts` (testing file)

2. **Component Class**: The component class (`header.component.ts`) contains the logic for the component, such as properties, methods, and lifecycle hooks.

```typescript
import { Component } from '@angular/core';

@Component({
    selector: 'app-header',
    templateUrl:
'./header.component.html',
```

```
        styleUrls: ['./header.component.css']
})
export class HeaderComponent {
    title: string = 'My Angular App';

    changeTitle() {
        this.title = 'Title Changed';
    }
}
```

3. **Template**: The template (header.component.html) defines the view and the layout of the component. It uses Angular's templating syntax to bind data and handle events.

html

```
<header>
    <h1>{{ title }}</h1>
    <button (click)="changeTitle()">Change
Title</button>
</header>
```

In this example, the title property is bound to the template using {{ title }}, and the changeTitle method is triggered when the button is clicked using the (click) event binding.

94

4. **Styles**: The component's styles are defined in the `header.component.css` file. These styles will be scoped to the `HeaderComponent`, meaning they won't affect other components in the application.

Real-World Example: Building a Basic Angular App

Now, let's build a simple Angular app where we display a list of items and allow users to add and remove items from the list.

1. **Generate the App Component**: Start with the default `app.component.ts` generated by Angular CLI. We'll modify it to manage the list of items.

2. **App Component Logic**: Modify the component to include an array of items and methods for adding and removing items.

```typescript
import { Component } from '@angular/core';

@Component({
    selector: 'app-root',
    templateUrl: './app.component.html',
    styleUrls: ['./app.component.css']
})
export class AppComponent {
```

```
items: string[] = ['Apple', 'Banana',
'Orange'];

addItem(newItem: string) {
    this.items.push(newItem);
}

removeItem(index: number) {
    this.items.splice(index, 1);
}
}
```

3. **App Component Template**: The HTML template will allow users to add and remove items from the list.

```html
html

<div>
    <h1>My Grocery List</h1>
    <ul>
        <li *ngFor="let item of items; let
i = index">
            {{ item }}
            <button
(click)="removeItem(i)">Remove</button>
        </li>
    </ul>
    <input     #newItem     type="text"
placeholder="Add item" />
```

```
<button
(click)="addItem(newItem.value)">Add</but
ton>
</div>
```

- o The `*ngFor` directive is used to loop over the `items` array and display each item in a list.
- o The `#newItem` template reference variable is used to get the input value for adding a new item.
- o The `removeItem` method is triggered when the "Remove" button is clicked, and it removes the corresponding item from the list.

4. **Run the Application**: Now, you can run the Angular app using `ng serve`. The app will display the grocery list and allow users to add or remove items.

In this chapter, we've introduced **Angular** as a full-featured framework for building dynamic web applications. We discussed how to set up Angular using the **Angular CLI**, created **components** and **templates**, and built a real-world example—a simple grocery list app. In the next chapter, we will explore **directives and data binding** in Angular, which are key to creating interactive and dynamic UIs.

CHAPTER 9

DIRECTIVES AND DATA BINDING IN ANGULAR

Understanding Angular Directives: ngIf, ngFor, etc.

In Angular, **directives** are special markers attached to DOM elements (tags, attributes, or classes) that modify their behavior or appearance. Directives allow you to extend HTML's functionality by applying logic and structure to the UI. Angular has three main types of directives: **Structural**, **Attribute**, and **Component** directives.

1. **Structural Directives**: These directives change the structure of the DOM by adding or removing elements. The most common structural directives are:
   - ○ `ngIf`: Conditionally includes an element in the DOM based on the truthiness of an expression. If the condition is true, the element is included; if false, it is removed.
   - ○ `ngFor`: Loops through an array and creates a new DOM element for each item in the array.

   Example of `ngIf`:

html

```
<div          *ngIf="isLoggedIn">Welcome,
User!</div>
<div *ngIf="!isLoggedIn">Please log in to
continue.</div>
```

In this example, the `ngIf` directive displays the first `div` if `isLoggedIn` is true, and the second `div` if `isLoggedIn` is false.

Example of `ngFor`:

html

```
<ul>
    <li *ngFor="let item of items">{{ item
}}</li>
</ul>
```

The `ngFor` directive loops over the `items` array and displays each item in an unordered list (`<ul>`). For each element in the `items` array, a new `<li>` is created.

2. **Attribute Directives**: These directives change the appearance or behavior of an element but do not affect its structure. Examples include:

    o **ngClass**: Adds or removes classes to/from an element.

      o   **ngStyle**: Adds or removes inline styles to/from an element.

Example of `ngClass`:

`html`

```
<div   [ngClass]="{   'active':   isActive,
'inactive': !isActive }">Status</div>
```

This directive dynamically adds the class `active` if `isActive` is true and `inactive` if `isActive` is false.

3. **Component Directives**: These directives are custom directives that create components. Every Angular component is essentially a directive with a template.

Two-Way Data Binding in Angular

In Angular, **data binding** refers to the synchronization of data between the component's state and the view (UI). Angular provides several types of data binding, including **one-way data binding** (from component to view) and **two-way data binding** (from component to view and view to component).

Two-way Data Binding allows both the component's state and the view to be synchronized. When the user changes the value in the UI, the component's state is updated. Similarly, when the component's state changes, the view is automatically updated.

Angular achieves two-way data binding using the **ngModel** directive. This is commonly used with form elements like `<input>`, `<select>`, and `<textarea>`.

Example of Two-Way Data Binding:

html

```
<input [(ngModel)]="username" placeholder="Enter
your name">
<p>Your username is: {{ username }}</p>
```

- **[(ngModel)]**: The combination of square brackets `[]` (one-way data binding) and parentheses `()` (event binding) allows both the component and the view to stay synchronized. When the user types in the input field, the `username` variable in the component is updated, and when the `username` variable is updated in the component, the input field reflects the change.

To use `ngModel`, you need to import the `FormsModule` from `@angular/forms` in your Angular module.

typescript

```
import { NgModule } from '@angular/core';
```

```
import { BrowserModule } from '@angular/platform-
browser';
import { FormsModule } from '@angular/forms';  //
Import FormsModule

@NgModule({
  imports: [BrowserModule, FormsModule], // Add
FormsModule to imports
  declarations: [AppComponent],
  bootstrap: [AppComponent]
})
export class AppModule { }
```

Real-World Example: Building an Interactive Form with Angular

Now, let's put everything together by building an interactive form where the user can input their name and email address. The form will use **two-way data binding** for the input fields, and we will use **ngIf** to conditionally display a success message after the form is submitted.

1. **Define the Component Logic**: In the component's TypeScript file (app.component.ts), we will create properties for the name, email, and form submission status.

   ```
   typescript
   ```

```
import { Component } from '@angular/core';

@Component({
    selector: 'app-root',
    templateUrl: './app.component.html',
    styleUrls: ['./app.component.css']
})
export class AppComponent {
    name: string = '';
    email: string = '';
    isFormSubmitted: boolean = false;

    submitForm() {
        this.isFormSubmitted = true;
    }
}
```

2. **Create the Template**: In the component's HTML file (app.component.html), we will bind the form fields to the component properties using **two-way data binding**. When the form is submitted, the submitForm() method will be called to update the isFormSubmitted flag.

```html
<div>
    <h1>Interactive Form</h1>
```

```
<form (ngSubmit)="submitForm()">
    <label for="name">Name:</label>
    <input            [(ngModel)]="name"
name="name" id="name" required />

    <label for="email">Email:</label>
    <input            [(ngModel)]="email"
name="email"    id="email"    type="email"
required />

    <button
type="submit">Submit</button>
  </form>

  <div *ngIf="isFormSubmitted">
    <p>Form                    submitted
successfully!</p>
    <p>Your name is: {{ name }}</p>
    <p>Your email is: {{ email }}</p>
  </div>
</div>
```

- o The **ngSubmit** directive listens for form submission and triggers the `submitForm()` method.
- o **[(ngModel)]** is used to create two-way data binding for the input fields, ensuring that the component's `name` and `email` properties stay synchronized with the input values.

- o ***ngIf** is used to conditionally display the success message and the submitted data once the form is submitted.

3. **Add Styles** (Optional): You can add some basic styles to make the form look nicer.

```css
css

form {
    display: flex;
    flex-direction: column;
    width: 300px;
    margin: 0 auto;
}

label {
    margin: 10px 0 5px;
}

input {
    padding: 8px;
    margin-bottom: 10px;
}

button {
    padding: 10px;
    background-color: #4CAF50;
    color: white;
    border: none;
```

105

```
        cursor: pointer;
}


button:hover {
    background-color: #45a049;
}


div {
    margin-top: 20px;
}
```

How It Works:

- When the user fills out the form and submits it, the `name` and `email` properties in the component are automatically updated using **two-way data binding**.

- The form is submitted using the **ngSubmit** directive, which calls the `submitForm()` method. This method sets the `isFormSubmitted` flag to `true`, triggering the ***ngIf** directive to show the success message and the submitted data.

- The form fields and success message stay in sync with the component's state, and the user can see the data they submitted immediately after submitting the form.

In this chapter, we explored **Angular directives** such as `ngIf` and `ngFor`, which allow us to manipulate the DOM and loop through data efficiently. We also covered **two-way data binding** with the `ngModel` directive, which enables seamless synchronization between the component state and the view. Finally, we built a real-world **interactive form** to demonstrate how these concepts work together in an Angular app. In the next chapter, we will dive into more advanced Angular topics such as **services** and **dependency injection**, which are essential for building scalable applications.

CHAPTER 10

SERVICES AND DEPENDENCY INJECTION IN ANGULAR

What are Angular Services and How Are They Used?

In Angular, **services** are classes that provide a specific functionality or data that can be shared across multiple components. Services are typically used for tasks such as fetching data from an API, handling business logic, or storing and sharing state between components.

Why use services?

- **Reusability**: Services allow you to write logic that can be reused across different components.
- **Separation of Concerns**: By moving business logic and data handling into services, components can focus solely on rendering the UI.
- **Testability**: Services make it easier to test your business logic because you can mock the services when testing components.

Services in Angular are usually singleton instances, meaning that they are created once and shared across components that depend on them.

To create a service in Angular, you can use Angular's CLI, which generates a service file, or you can manually create a service class.

Understanding Dependency Injection

Dependency Injection (DI) is a design pattern that allows Angular to manage the instances of services and inject them into components or other services as dependencies. Instead of manually creating an instance of a service within a component, Angular provides the service to the component automatically.

Angular's DI system is powerful and helps you:

- **Decouple components and services**: Components do not need to create or manage the service instances themselves.
- **Improve testability**: By injecting services, you can easily replace services with mocks or stubs in tests.

In Angular, when you need to use a service in a component, you **inject** the service into the component's constructor. Angular's DI system will then handle the creation and injection of the service.

How to Create and Use a Service in Angular

1. **Create a Service**: You can generate a service using Angular CLI:

   ```bash
   bash
   ```

   ```bash
   ng generate service data
   ```

   This will generate a file `data.service.ts` with a basic service template.

2. **Define the Service**: Inside the service file (`data.service.ts`), you define the service's functionality. For example, you might have a service that fetches data from an API:

   ```typescript
   typescript
   ```

   ```typescript
   import { Injectable } from '@angular/core';
   import { HttpClient } from '@angular/common/http';
   import { Observable } from 'rxjs';

   @Injectable({
       providedIn: 'root'
   })
   ```

110

```
export class DataService {
    private              apiUrl              =
'https://api.example.com/data';

    constructor(private  http:  HttpClient)
{}

    getData(): Observable<any> {
        return this.http.get(this.apiUrl);
    }
}
```

- o **@Injectable()** **Decorator**: The `@Injectable()` decorator tells Angular that this service can be injected into components and other services. The `providedIn: 'root'` option ensures that the service is a singleton and available throughout the application.
- o **HttpClient**: The `HttpClient` module is used to make HTTP requests. In this case, the `getData()` method makes a GET request to the API and returns an `Observable`.

3. **Inject the Service into a Component**: Now, let's use the service in a component. You inject the service into the component's constructor, and then use it in the component's logic.

```
typescript
```

```
import { Component, OnInit } from
'@angular/core';
import { DataService } from
'./data.service';

@Component({
    selector: 'app-root',
    templateUrl: './app.component.html',
    styleUrls: ['./app.component.css']
})
export class AppComponent implements
OnInit {
    data: any;

    constructor(private        dataService:
DataService) {}

    ngOnInit(): void {

this.dataService.getData().subscribe(
            (response) => {
                this.data = response;
            },
            (error) => {
                console.error('Error
fetching data', error);
            }
        );
```

```
      }
}
```

- o **Injection in Constructor**: The `DataService` is injected into the `AppComponent` constructor.

- o **Fetching Data**: In the `ngOnInit()` lifecycle hook, the `getData()` method from the service is called. The component subscribes to the `Observable` returned by the service to get the data.

- o **Handling the Response**: The data is stored in the `data` property, which can be used in the template to display the fetched data.

Real-World Example: Creating a Service for Fetching Data from an API

Let's extend the example to create a complete Angular app that fetches data from an API and displays it in the component. In this case, we will fetch a list of users from a sample API (`https://jsonplaceholder.typicode.com/users`).

1. **Create the Data Service**: First, generate the service that will handle the API call:

bash

```
ng generate service user
```

Then, in `user.service.ts`, define the service that will fetch user data:

```typescript
import { Injectable } from '@angular/core';
import { HttpClient } from '@angular/common/http';
import { Observable } from 'rxjs';

@Injectable({
    providedIn: 'root'
})
export class UserService {
    private apiUrl = 'https://jsonplaceholder.typicode.com/users';

    constructor(private http: HttpClient) {}

    getUsers(): Observable<any> {
        return this.http.get(this.apiUrl);
    }
}
```

2. **Modify the Component to Use the Service**: Inject the `UserService` into the component and call `getUsers()` to fetch the user data.

In `app.component.ts`:

typescript

```
import { Component, OnInit } from
'@angular/core';
import { UserService } from
'./user.service';

@Component({
    selector: 'app-root',
    templateUrl: './app.component.html',
    styleUrls: ['./app.component.css']
})
export class AppComponent implements
OnInit {
    users: any[] = [];

    constructor(private      userService:
UserService) {}

    ngOnInit(): void {

this.userService.getUsers().subscribe(
            (data) => {
```

```
                this.users = data;
        },
        (error) => {
                console.error('Error
fetching users', error);
        }
    );
  }
}
```

3. **Display the Data in the Template**: Now, display the fetched user data in the template (`app.component.html`):

html

```html
<h1>User List</h1>

<ul *ngIf="users.length > 0; else loading">
    <li *ngFor="let user of users">
        <h3>{{ user.name }}</h3>
        <p>{{ user.email }}</p>
    </li>
</ul>

<ng-template #loading>
    <p>Loading users...</p>
</ng-template>
```

116

- o ***ngFor**: The `*ngFor` directive loops over the `users` array and displays each user's name and email.
- o ***ngIf with ng-template**: If the `users` array is empty, the loading message is displayed using `*ngIf` with an `ng-template`. Once the data is fetched, the list of users is shown.

4. **Run the Application**: Finally, start the development server:

```bash

ng serve
```

The application will fetch the user data from the API and display the list of users in the UI.

Key Points:

- **Services**: Angular services are used to handle logic and data fetching, making it easier to share data between components.
- **Dependency Injection**: Angular's DI system allows services to be injected into components, enabling better code modularity and testability.

- **Real-World Example**: In this example, we created a service to fetch data from an API and used it in a component to display a list of users.

In this chapter, we covered the creation and usage of Angular services, how dependency injection works in Angular, and built a real-world example of fetching and displaying data using services. In the next chapter, we will explore **routing in Angular**, which will allow us to navigate between different views in a single-page application.

CHAPTER 11

ROUTING IN ANGULAR

Setting Up Routing in an Angular App

Routing in Angular allows you to navigate between different views or pages within a single-page application (SPA) without reloading the entire page. Angular's routing module provides tools for defining routes, managing navigation, and controlling the user experience as they move through your app.

To set up routing in an Angular application, follow these steps:

1. **Import Angular Router Module**: Angular has a dedicated module for routing called `@angular/router`. To enable routing in your app, first import `RouterModule` and configure the routes in the main application module (`app.module.ts`).

   typescript

   ```
   import { NgModule } from '@angular/core';
   import { BrowserModule } from '@angular/platform-browser';
   ```

```
import    {    RouterModule    }    from
'@angular/router';
import    {    AppComponent    }    from
'./app.component';
import    {    HomeComponent    }    from
'./home/home.component';
import    {    AboutComponent    }    from
'./about/about.component';

@NgModule({
  declarations:             [AppComponent,
HomeComponent, AboutComponent],
  imports: [
    BrowserModule,
    RouterModule.forRoot([
      { path: '', component: HomeComponent
},
      {    path:    'about',    component:
AboutComponent }
    ])
  ],
  providers: [],
  bootstrap: [AppComponent]
})
export class AppModule {}
```

In this example:

  o `RouterModule.forRoot()` configures the routes for the application. Each route is defined by a `path` (URL segment) and a corresponding `component` that will be displayed when that route is matched.

2. **Define Routes**: In the `RouterModule.forRoot()` method, you define the routes for the application. In this case, the app has two routes:

  o The home route (`''`) which renders the `HomeComponent`.

  o The about route (`'about'`) which renders the `AboutComponent`.

3. **Add Router Outlet**: The router outlet is the placeholder where the routed components will be displayed. In the `app.component.html`, add the `<router-outlet>` directive:

html

```html
<div>
  <h1>My Angular App</h1>
  <nav>
    <a routerLink="/">Home</a>
    <a routerLink="/about">About</a>
  </nav>
  <router-outlet></router-outlet>
</div>
```

The `routerLink` directive is used to create links that trigger navigation when clicked. The `<router-outlet>` is where the routed components will be injected.

4. **Create the Components**: Ensure you have the components defined, such as `HomeComponent` and `AboutComponent`, either manually or by using Angular CLI.

Understanding Routes, Navigation, and Guards

1. **Routes**: A route in Angular defines a path and a component that should be displayed when that path is matched. The route configuration can also include additional features such as route parameters, query parameters, and more.

   Example of defining a route with a parameter:

   ```typescript
   { path: 'user/:id', component: UserComponent }
   ```

122

In this case, `:id` is a dynamic route parameter that can be accessed inside the component as part of the activated route.

2. **Navigation**: Navigation refers to the act of moving from one route to another. In Angular, navigation can be triggered by either using the `routerLink` directive (for declarative navigation) or the `Router` service (for programmatic navigation).

   o **Declarative Navigation**: The `routerLink` directive is used in the template to define navigation links.

   html

   ```html
   <a routerLink="/about">Go to About Page</a>
   ```

   o **Programmatic Navigation**: You can navigate to a route programmatically using Angular's `Router` service.

   typescript

   ```typescript
   import { Router } from '@angular/router';
   ```

```
constructor(private router: Router)
{}

navigateToAbout() {

this.router.navigate(['/about']);
}
```

3. **Route Guards**: Route guards are used to control access to routes based on certain conditions, such as whether a user is logged in or has the necessary permissions. Angular provides several types of guards:

    o   **CanActivate**: Decides if a route can be activated (e.g., checking if a user is authenticated).

    o   **CanDeactivate**: Decides if a route can be deactivated (e.g., warning the user before leaving a page with unsaved changes).

    o   **CanLoad**: Decides if a module can be loaded (e.g., checking if the user has access to a feature before loading the module).

Example of a **CanActivate** guard:

```typescript
import { Injectable } from '@angular/core';
import            {            CanActivate,
ActivatedRouteSnapshot,
```

```
RouterStateSnapshot,    Router    }    from
'@angular/router';
import    {    AuthService    }    from
'./auth.service';

@Injectable({
  providedIn: 'root'
})
export    class    AuthGuard    implements
CanActivate {
  constructor(private          authService:
AuthService, private router: Router) {}

  canActivate(
    route: ActivatedRouteSnapshot,
    state: RouterStateSnapshot
  ): boolean {
    if (this.authService.isLoggedIn()) {
      return true;
    } else {
      this.router.navigate(['/login']);
      return false;
    }
  }
}
```

In this example, the `AuthGuard` checks if the user is logged in before allowing them to access a route. If the user is not logged in, they are redirected to the login page.

You can apply guards to a route by using the `canActivate` property in the route configuration:

```typescript
{ path: 'profile', component:
ProfileComponent, canActivate: [AuthGuard]
}
```

Real-World Example: Building a Multi-Page Angular App with Route Guards

Let's now build a real-world example of an Angular app with multiple routes and route guards. In this example, we will create a basic authentication flow where users need to be logged in to access certain pages.

1. **Create Components**: Generate the necessary components using Angular CLI.

    ```bash
    ng generate component login
    ng generate component dashboard
    ng generate component home
    ```

2. **AuthGuard**: Implement a simple `AuthGuard` to protect the `dashboard` route.

```typescript
import { Injectable } from '@angular/core';
import { CanActivate } from '@angular/router';
import { Router } from '@angular/router';

@Injectable({
  providedIn: 'root'
})
export class AuthGuard implements CanActivate {
  constructor(private router: Router) {}

  canActivate(): boolean {
    const isLoggedIn = localStorage.getItem('isLoggedIn');
    if (isLoggedIn === 'true') {
      return true;
    } else {
      this.router.navigate(['/login']);
      return false;
    }
  }
}
```

3. **Routing Configuration**: In `app.module.ts`, configure the routes, applying the `AuthGuard` to the `dashboard` route.

127

```typescript
import { NgModule } from '@angular/core';
import { RouterModule, Routes } from '@angular/router';
import { HomeComponent } from './home/home.component';
import { LoginComponent } from './login/login.component';
import { DashboardComponent } from './dashboard/dashboard.component';
import { AuthGuard } from './auth.guard';

const routes: Routes = [
  { path: '', component: HomeComponent },
  { path: 'login', component: LoginComponent },
  { path: 'dashboard', component: DashboardComponent, canActivate: [AuthGuard] }
];

@NgModule({
  imports: [RouterModule.forRoot(routes)],
  exports: [RouterModule]
})
export class AppRoutingModule {}
```

4. **Login Component**: In the `login.component.ts`, create a simple login method that sets `isLoggedIn` in `localStorage`.

typescript

```
import { Component } from '@angular/core';
import { Router } from '@angular/router';

@Component({
  selector: 'app-login',
  templateUrl: './login.component.html',
  styleUrls: ['./login.component.css']
})
export class LoginComponent {
  constructor(private router: Router) {}

  login() {
    localStorage.setItem('isLoggedIn',
'true');
    this.router.navigate(['/dashboard']);
  }
}
```

The `login()` method sets `isLoggedIn` to `'true'` and redirects the user to the `dashboard` page.

5. **Dashboard Component**: The `dashboard.component.html` will display a simple message:

html

```
<h2>Welcome to the Dashboard!</h2>
```

6. **Home Component**: The `home.component.html` will include a link to the login page:

html

```
<h1>Welcome to our App</h1>
<p><a routerLink="/login">Go to Login</a></p>
```

How It Works:

- **Routing**: The app has three pages—Home, Login, and Dashboard. The `Dashboard` route is protected by the `AuthGuard`, ensuring that only authenticated users can access it.

- **Route Guard**: When the user tries to access the `Dashboard` page, the `AuthGuard` checks if `isLoggedIn` is stored in `localStorage`. If it's not, the user is redirected to the Login page.

- **Navigation**: The user can navigate between pages using the `routerLink` directive, and programmatically via the `Router` service.

In this chapter, we explored **Angular routing**, how to configure routes and navigation, and how to use **route guards** to protect sensitive pages. We also built a real-world example with multiple pages and implemented an authentication flow using route guards. In the next chapter, we will dive into **Angular forms**, including template-driven and reactive forms, to handle user input more effectively.

CHAPTER 12

FORMS IN ANGULAR: TEMPLATE-DRIVEN AND REACTIVE FORMS

Understanding Template-Driven Forms vs Reactive Forms

In Angular, there are two main ways to handle forms: **Template-Driven Forms** and **Reactive Forms**. Both approaches allow you to collect and manage user input, but they differ in how the form is structured and managed. Each approach has its use cases and advantages.

Template-Driven Forms

Template-driven forms are easy to use and are defined directly in the HTML template. Angular automatically binds the form controls to the component's properties using directives like `ngModel`, `ngForm`, and others. This approach is ideal for simple forms where you don't need much business logic or advanced form validation.

Key Features:

- **Simple Syntax**: Template-driven forms use Angular directives in the HTML template to define the form and its controls.
- **Two-Way Binding**: Form controls are connected to the component properties using `ngModel`, which provides two-way data binding.
- **Easy to Set Up**: Ideal for smaller forms and when simplicity is a priority.
- **Limited Validation**: Validation logic is generally simple and mostly defined in the template.

Example of a Template-Driven Form:

html

```
<form                      #loginForm="ngForm"
(ngSubmit)="onSubmit(loginForm)">
    <div>
        <label for="email">Email:</label>
        <input      type="email"      id="email"
name="email" ngModel required>
    </div>
    <div>
        <label for="password">Password:</label>
        <input    type="password"    id="password"
name="password" ngModel required>
    </div>
```

```
<button                              type="submit"
[disabled]="!loginForm.valid">Login</button>
</form>
```

In the example above:

- `ngModel` is used to bind the form inputs to component properties.
- The `ngForm` directive is used to manage the entire form's state and validation.
- Validation is handled through the `required` attribute and Angular's built-in form validation.

Reactive Forms

Reactive forms are more flexible and scalable, and they are defined entirely in the component class using `FormControl`, `FormGroup`, and `FormBuilder`. This approach is more suitable for complex forms where you need fine-grained control over the form's structure, validation, and behavior.

Key Features:

- **Explicit Form Model**: The form is defined and managed entirely in the component class. Form controls are created programmatically using `FormControl`, `FormGroup`, and `FormBuilder`.

134

- **Synchronous Validation**: You can define custom validation logic and synchronous validation functions in the component class.
- **More Control**: Reactive forms offer more control over the form state and validation.
- **Better for Large Forms**: They are well-suited for dynamic forms or forms with complex validation rules.

Example of a Reactive Form:

typescript

```
import { Component, OnInit } from
'@angular/core';
import { FormBuilder, FormGroup, Validators }
from '@angular/forms';

@Component({
    selector: 'app-login',
    templateUrl: './login.component.html',
})
export class LoginComponent implements OnInit {
    loginForm: FormGroup;

    constructor(private fb: FormBuilder) {}

    ngOnInit(): void {
        this.loginForm = this.fb.group({
            email: ['', [Validators.required,
Validators.email]],
```

135

```
        password: ['', [Validators.required,
Validators.minLength(6)]],
      });
  }


  onSubmit(): void {
      if (this.loginForm.valid) {
          console.log(this.loginForm.value);
      }
  }
}
```
html

```html
<form                    [formGroup]="loginForm"
(ngSubmit)="onSubmit()">
    <div>
        <label for="email">Email:</label>
        <input      type="email"      id="email"
formControlName="email">
        <div
*ngIf="loginForm.get('email').invalid        &&
loginForm.get('email').touched">
            <small    class="error">Email    is
required and must be valid</small>
        </div>
    </div>
    <div>
        <label for="password">Password:</label>
```

```
        <input   type="password"   id="password"
formControlName="password">
        <div
*ngIf="loginForm.get('password').invalid      &&
loginForm.get('password').touched">
            <small   class="error">Password   is
required  and  must  be  at  least  6  characters
long</small>
        </div>
    </div>
    <button                       type="submit"
[disabled]="loginForm.invalid">Login</button>
</form>
```

In the example above:

- The `FormBuilder` service is used to create the form group and form controls programmatically.
- Validation is defined in the component class using `Validators` such as `required`, `email`, and `minLength`.
- The form state (e.g., validity, touched) is checked in the template to display validation messages.

Key Differences Between Template-Driven and Reactive Forms

137

Feature	Template-Driven Forms	Reactive Forms
Form Model	Defined in the template	Defined in the component
Complexity	Simple and easy to use	More powerful and flexible
Validation	Simple validation via template directives	Synchronous, more flexible validation
Form Control Setup	Automatically done by Angular	Explicitly defined in the component
Dynamic Forms	Less suitable for dynamic forms	Best suited for dynamic forms
Scalability	Better for simple forms	Better for complex forms

Form Validation and Handling User Inputs

Both template-driven and reactive forms support form validation. However, the validation process is slightly different for each approach.

1. **Template-Driven Validation**: You can use built-in validators like `required`, `minlength`, and `maxlength` in the template. These validators can be combined with custom validation functions.

   Example:

   html

   ```
   <input type="text" name="username" ngModel
   required minlength="5">
   <div *ngIf="form.controls.username.invalid
   && form.controls.username.touched">
       <small
   *ngIf="form.controls.username.errors?.req
   uired">Username is required.</small>
       <small
   *ngIf="form.controls.username.errors?.min
   length">Username must be at least 5
   characters long.</small>
   </div>
   ```

2. **Reactive Form Validation**: Validation is done in the component class using `FormControl` and `Validators`. You can easily add custom validation logic or async validation if necessary.

   Example:

139

```typescript
typescript

this.loginForm = this.fb.group({
    username: ['', [Validators.required,
Validators.minLength(5)]],
});
```

In the template, you can then check the validity of each form control:

```html
html

<input formControlName="username">
<div
*ngIf="loginForm.controls.username.invali
d && loginForm.controls.username.touched">
    <small
*ngIf="loginForm.controls.username.errors
?.required">Username is required.</small>
    <small
*ngIf="loginForm.controls.username.errors
?.minlength">Username must be at least 5
characters long.</small>
</div>
```

Real-World Example: Building a Login and Registration Form

Let's create a simple **login** and **registration** form using both **template-driven** and **reactive forms**.

1. **Login Form Using Template-Driven Approach**:

```html
<form                    #loginForm="ngForm"
(ngSubmit)="onSubmit(loginForm)">
    <label for="email">Email:</label>
    <input     type="email"     id="email"
name="email" ngModel required>

    <label
for="password">Password:</label>
    <input type="password" id="password"
name="password" ngModel required>

    <button                   type="submit"
[disabled]="!loginForm.valid">Login</butt
on>
</form>
```

2. **Login Form Using Reactive Approach**:

```typescript
export class LoginComponent {
    loginForm: FormGroup;
```

```
    constructor(private   fb:   FormBuilder)
{}

    ngOnInit() {
        this.loginForm = this.fb.group({
            email:                    ['',
[Validators.required, Validators.email]],
            password:                 ['',
[Validators.required,
Validators.minLength(6)]]
        });
    }

    onSubmit() {
        if (this.loginForm.valid) {
            console.log('Form       Data:',
this.loginForm.value);
        }
    }
}
html

<form              [formGroup]="loginForm"
(ngSubmit)="onSubmit()">
    <label for="email">Email:</label>
    <input          formControlName="email"
type="email">
```

```
    <label
for="password">Password:</label>
    <input        formControlName="password"
type="password">

    <button                type="submit"
[disabled]="loginForm.invalid">Login</but
ton>
</form>
```

3. **Registration Form Using Reactive Approach**:

```typescript
export class RegisterComponent {
    registerForm: FormGroup;

    constructor(private fb: FormBuilder)
{}

    ngOnInit() {
        this.registerForm               =
this.fb.group({
            name:                  ['',
[Validators.required,
Validators.minLength(3)]],
            email:                 ['',
[Validators.required, Validators.email]],
```

```
        password:                ['',
[Validators.required,
Validators.minLength(6)]],
        confirmPassword:         ['',
[Validators.required]]
    }, {
      validator:
this.passwordMatchValidator
    });
  }


  passwordMatchValidator(group:
FormGroup) {
    const      password      =
group.get('password').value;
    const    confirmPassword    =
group.get('confirmPassword').value;
    return      password      ===
confirmPassword ? null : { mismatch: true
};
  }


  onSubmit() {
    if (this.registerForm.valid) {
      console.log('Registration
Data:', this.registerForm.value);
    }
  }
}
```

144

html

```html
<form [formGroup]="registerForm"
(ngSubmit)="onSubmit()">
    <label for="name">Name:</label>
    <input formControlName="name">

    <label for="email">Email:</label>
    <input formControlName="email">

    <label
for="password">Password:</label>
    <input formControlName="password"
type="password">

    <label for="confirmPassword">Confirm
Password:</label>
    <input
formControlName="confirmPassword"
type="password">

    <button type="submit"
[disabled]="registerForm.invalid">Registe
r</button>
</form>
```

145

Summary:

- **Template-Driven Forms**: Simple and declarative, ideal for smaller forms. Form validation and model binding are handled directly in the template.
- **Reactive Forms**: More powerful and flexible, suitable for complex forms. The form model is defined programmatically in the component.
- **Validation**: Both approaches support form validation, with reactive forms offering more control over validation logic and asynchronous validation.
- **Real-World Example**: We created login and registration forms using both methods, demonstrating how Angular forms work in practice.

In the next chapter, we will explore **Angular's HTTP Client** for making API requests and handling asynchronous data in your applications.

CHAPTER 13

ADVANCED ANGULAR: OBSERVABLES AND RXJS

Introduction to Observables and Why They're Important

In Angular, **Observables** are used to handle asynchronous operations such as HTTP requests, user inputs, or timers. They are a core part of Angular's reactive programming model, enabling developers to work with streams of data over time.

An **Observable** represents a collection of future values or events, and it allows you to subscribe to those values. Instead of relying on callbacks or promises, Observables provide a more powerful and flexible way to manage asynchronous data.

Why Are Observables Important?

1. **Asynchronous Data Handling**: Observables allow you to handle asynchronous events, such as data coming from a server, user input, or WebSocket messages, in a declarative manner.
2. **Composability**: Observables can be combined using **RxJS operators** (like `map`, `filter`, `merge`, and

147

`switchMap`) to transform, filter, or combine streams of data in a clean and readable way.

3. **Cancellation**: Observables provide built-in support for canceling subscriptions when data is no longer needed, helping manage resources more efficiently.

4. **Event Handling**: Since Observables can represent any stream of events (like mouse clicks, key presses, etc.), they are a perfect fit for handling UI events in Angular.

Core Concepts of Observables:

- **Observer**: An object that receives notifications from the Observable.

- **Subscription**: An object that represents the execution of the Observable. You use it to manage the lifecycle of the Observable, such as unsubscribing when no longer needed.

- **Operator**: Functions that transform, filter, or combine Observables. Examples include `map`, `filter`, `mergeMap`, `switchMap`, and more.

- **Subject**: A type of Observable that allows values to be multicasted to many Observers.

Using RxJS Operators for Managing Asynchronous Data

RxJS (Reactive Extensions for JavaScript) is a powerful library that provides a set of operators for working with Observables. RxJS operators are essential when it comes to transforming and managing asynchronous data in Angular applications. They allow you to manipulate data streams in a functional and declarative style.

Commonly Used RxJS Operators:

1. **map()**: Transforms each emitted value by applying a function to it.

   ```typescript
   import { of } from 'rxjs';
   import { map } from 'rxjs/operators';

   const observable = of(1, 2, 3);
   observable.pipe(
       map(value => value * 2)
   ).subscribe(console.log); // Outputs: 2, 4, 6
   ```

2. **filter()**: Filters emitted values based on a condition.

   ```typescript
   import { of } from 'rxjs';
   import { filter } from 'rxjs/operators';
   ```

149

```
const observable = of(1, 2, 3, 4, 5);
observable.pipe(
    filter(value => value % 2 === 0)
).subscribe(console.log); // Outputs: 2, 4
```

3. **switchMap()**: Switches to a new Observable, canceling the previous one if a new value is emitted.

typescript

```
import { of } from 'rxjs';
import { switchMap } from 'rxjs/operators';

const observable = of('first', 'second');
observable.pipe(
    switchMap(value => {
        return of(`${value} transformed`);
    })
).subscribe(console.log);    //    Outputs:
first transformed, second transformed
```

4. **mergeMap()**: Flattens multiple inner Observables into a single Observable.

typescript

```
import { of } from 'rxjs';
import { mergeMap } from 'rxjs/operators';
```

```
const observable = of(1, 2, 3);
observable.pipe(
    mergeMap(value => of(value * 2))
).subscribe(console.log);  // Outputs:  2,
4, 6
```

5. **catchError()**: Catches errors in an Observable and allows you to handle them.

```typescript
import { of } from 'rxjs';
import       {       catchError       }       from
'rxjs/operators';

const observable = of(1, 2, 3);
observable.pipe(
    catchError(err => {
        console.error('Error:', err);
        return of('Error handled');
    })
).subscribe(console.log);  // Outputs:  1,
2, 3
```

Creating and Using Observables in Angular:

In Angular, Observables are commonly used for tasks such as handling HTTP requests, responding to form inputs, or managing event streams. Angular's `HttpClient` service, for example, returns Observables that can be subscribed to for handling responses from API calls.

Real-World Example: Handling HTTP Requests with RxJS

In this example, we'll create a simple Angular service that makes an HTTP request to fetch a list of users from an API and processes the response using RxJS operators.

1. **Setup the Angular Service**: First, let's create a service that uses Angular's `HttpClient` to make HTTP requests. You can generate the service using Angular CLI:

   ```bash
   bash
   ```

   ```bash
   ng generate service user
   ```

2. **User Service Implementation**: Inside `user.service.ts`, import `HttpClient` and use it to fetch data from an API. The `getUsers()` method will return an Observable.

   ```typescript
   typescript
   ```

   ```typescript
   import { Injectable } from '@angular/core';
   import { HttpClient } from
   '@angular/common/http';
   ```

152

```
import { Observable } from 'rxjs';
import { map, catchError } from
'rxjs/operators';

@Injectable({
    providedIn: 'root'
})
export class UserService {
    private apiUrl =
'https://jsonplaceholder.typicode.com/use
rs';

    constructor(private http: HttpClient)
{}

    getUsers(): Observable<any> {
        return
this.http.get(this.apiUrl).pipe(
            map(response => response),  //
You can transform the response here
            catchError(error => {
                console.error('Error
fetching users:', error);
                throw error;  // Handle
errors properly in real apps
            })
        );
    }
}
```

- o **get()**: The `http.get()` method returns an Observable that emits the response from the API.
- o **map()**: The `map` operator transforms the response if necessary.
- o **catchError()**: The `catchError` operator handles any errors that may occur during the request.

3. **Using the Service in a Component**: Next, use this service in a component to fetch and display the list of users.

typescript

```typescript
import { Component, OnInit } from
'@angular/core';
import { UserService } from
'./user.service';

@Component({
    selector: 'app-user-list',
    templateUrl:                '. /user-
list.component.html',
    styleUrls:                  ['. /user-
list.component.css']
})
export class UserListComponent implements
OnInit {
    users: any[] = [];
```

```
    constructor(private        userService:
UserService) {}


    ngOnInit(): void {

this.userService.getUsers().subscribe(
        (data) => {
            this.users = data;
        },
        (error) => {
            console.error('Error
loading users:', error);
        }
        );
    }
}
```

4. **Display Data in the Template**: In user-list.component.html, use *ngFor to display the list of users.

```html
<h1>User List</h1>
<ul>
    <li *ngFor="let user of users">
        <h3>{{ user.name }}</h3>
        <p>Email: {{ user.email }}</p>
```

155

```
</li>
</ul>
```

5. **Error Handling**: If there's an error with the HTTP request (e.g., no internet connection or the API is down), the `catchError` operator in the service will catch the error. You can handle it gracefully by showing an error message to the user.

Key Points:

- **Observables**: In Angular, Observables allow you to manage asynchronous data streams, and RxJS operators provide powerful tools for transforming and handling this data.

- **RxJS Operators**: Operators like `map`, `filter`, `mergeMap`, and `switchMap` make it easy to manipulate data streams in a declarative way.

- **HttpClient**: The `HttpClient` service in Angular returns Observables for HTTP requests. You can use operators like `map` and `catchError` to handle the response and manage errors.

- **Real-World Example**: We created a user service to fetch data from an API and displayed the data in a component. We also implemented error handling using `catchError`.

In the next chapter, we will explore **Angular modules** and how to organize an Angular application into cohesive units for better maintainability and scalability.

CHAPTER 14

ANGULAR CLI AND PROJECT STRUCTURE

Understanding Angular CLI Commands

The **Angular CLI** (Command Line Interface) is a powerful tool that helps Angular developers automate tasks such as project setup, development, testing, building, and deployment. The CLI provides a set of commands to make your development process faster and more efficient, offering functionality for generating components, services, modules, and more.

Here are some commonly used Angular CLI commands:

1. **Creating a New Angular Project**: The `ng new` command is used to create a new Angular project. It sets up a new project with all the necessary files, dependencies, and configuration.

```bash
```

```
ng new my-angular-app
```

158

You can customize the project setup by adding flags, such as:

- o `--routing`: Adds routing capabilities.
- o `--style=scss`: Specifies the stylesheet format (CSS, SCSS, etc.).

2. **Running the Development Server**: Once your project is set up, use `ng serve` to run the development server. The app will be available at `http://localhost:4200/`.

```bash

ng serve
```

3. **Generating Components, Services, Modules, etc.**: The `ng generate` or `ng g` command is used to generate various Angular elements like components, services, pipes, and modules.

- o Generate a component:

```bash

ng generate component component-name
```

- o Generate a service:

```bash

ng generate service service-name
```

159

    o   Generate a module:

```bash
```

```
ng generate module module-name
```

4. This helps in maintaining a clean and organized project structure, as the CLI automatically generates the files and folders with the correct naming conventions.

5. **Building the Project for Production**: The `ng build` command compiles the Angular application into an optimized production build.

```bash
```

```
ng build --prod
```

This will create a `dist/` folder with the production-ready files, minified and optimized for deployment.

6. **Running Tests**: Angular CLI integrates with Jasmine and Karma for unit testing. You can run your tests with the following command:

```bash
```

```
ng test
```

7. **Running End-to-End Tests**: Angular uses Protractor for end-to-end testing. Use the following command to run your end-to-end tests:

```bash
ng e2e
```

These are just a few of the many commands available in Angular CLI, making it easier for developers to maintain their workflow and keep the application organized.

Setting Up and Managing Angular Projects

Angular CLI helps you quickly set up and manage Angular projects by automating tedious tasks and enforcing best practices. When you create an Angular project, it comes with a set of default folders and files that structure the application. This structure ensures that the application is scalable and easy to manage as it grows.

Here's an overview of the standard project structure:

1. **src/**: This is where the core application code resides.
    - **app/**: Contains the main application files, including components, services, and modules.

o **assets/**: Stores static assets like images, fonts, and styles.

o **environments/**: Holds environment configuration files (environment.ts for development, environment.prod.ts for production).

2. **angular.json**: This file contains the Angular workspace configuration, including settings for building, serving, testing, and deploying the app.

3. **package.json**: The project's package.json file manages dependencies, scripts, and metadata.

4. **tsconfig.json**: The TypeScript configuration file, defining settings for TypeScript compilation.

5. **karma.conf.js**: The configuration file for Karma, the test runner used by Angular CLI.

6. **protractor.conf.js**: The configuration file for Protractor, used for end-to-end testing.

This setup is intended to keep the project well-organized as it grows in size, with each feature or module separated into its own directory within the src/app/ folder.

Best Practices for Organizing Files and Folders

To maintain a clean and scalable Angular project, it's important to organize files and folders logically. Here are some best practices for organizing Angular projects:

1. **Feature-Based Structure**: Organize your app into modules and components based on features rather than technical concepts (like "services" or "models"). For example, a "User" feature might have a module with a component, service, and routing configuration specific to user management.

   text

   ```
   src/
   ├── app/
   │   ├── user/
   │   │   ├── user.module.ts
   │   │   ├── user.component.ts
   │   │   ├── user.service.ts
   │   │   ├── user-routing.module.ts
   │   │   └── user.model.ts
   │   ├── auth/
   │   │   ├── auth.module.ts
   │   │   ├── login.component.ts
   │   │   └── auth.service.ts
   ```

2. **Keep Services and Components Together**: For small features or components, it's a good practice to keep the component and its related service within the same folder.

This helps in organizing the app by feature and avoids scattering code across the project.

```text
src/
├── app/
│   ├── dashboard/
│   │   ├── dashboard.component.ts
│   │   ├── dashboard.service.ts
│   │   └── dashboard.component.html
```

3. **Shared Modules**: For shared functionality like custom directives, pipes, or components used across different parts of the app, create a shared module.

```text
src/
├── app/
│   ├── shared/
│   │   ├── shared.module.ts
│   │   ├── spinner.component.ts
│   │   ├── capitalize.pipe.ts
│   │   └── validation.directive.ts
```

4. **Lazy Loading with Modules**: For large applications, use **lazy loading** to load specific modules only when they are

needed. This keeps the initial bundle size small and improves app performance.

Define a lazy-loaded module in your routing:

```typescript
const routes: Routes = [
  { path: 'user', loadChildren: () => import('./user/user.module').then(m => m.UserModule) },
];
```

The `UserModule` will only be loaded when the user navigates to `/user`.

Real-World Example: Building a Feature-Rich Angular App Using the CLI

Let's build a basic Angular app using the CLI to demonstrate setting up and managing Angular projects.

1. **Create a New Project**: Generate a new Angular project using the following command:

   ```bash
   ```

```
ng new feature-rich-app
```

During the creation, enable routing and choose the stylesheet format (CSS, SCSS, etc.).

2. **Generate Modules and Components**: Create modules and components for different features like `user` and `auth`.

```bash
ng generate module user --routing
ng generate component user/user-list
ng generate service user/user
```

Similarly, create an `auth` module for user authentication:

```bash
ng generate module auth --routing
ng generate component auth/login
ng generate service auth/auth
```

3. **Implement Routing for User and Auth**: Set up routes to lazy-load the `user` and `auth` modules. In `app-routing.module.ts`:

```typescript
```

```
const routes: Routes = [
  { path: '', redirectTo: '/home',
pathMatch: 'full' },
  { path: 'user', loadChildren: () =>
import('./user/user.module').then(m =>
m.UserModule) },
  { path: 'auth', loadChildren: () =>
import('./auth/auth.module').then(m =>
m.AuthModule) },
];
```

4. **Add Authentication Flow**: In the auth/login.component.ts, implement the login functionality using Angular forms and a mock authentication service.

```typescript
```

```
import { Component } from '@angular/core';
import { Router } from '@angular/router';
import { AuthService } from
'./auth.service';

@Component({
  selector: 'app-login',
  templateUrl: './login.component.html',
})
export class LoginComponent {
```

```
constructor(private          authService:
AuthService, private router: Router) {}


login() {
  this.authService.login().subscribe(()
=> {
    this.router.navigate(['/user']);
  });
}
}
```

5. **Display User List**: In the `user/user-list.component.ts`, fetch the list of users from the `user.service.ts` and display it.

typescript

```
import { Component, OnInit } from
'@angular/core';
import { UserService } from
'./user.service';

@Component({
  selector: 'app-user-list',
  templateUrl:              './user-list.component.html',
})
export class UserListComponent implements
OnInit {
```

```
users: any[] = [];

constructor(private          userService:
UserService) {}

ngOnInit() {

this.userService.getUsers().subscribe(dat
a => {
    this.users = data;
  });
}
}
```

Key Takeaways:

- **Angular CLI**: Angular CLI simplifies many aspects of project setup, development, and deployment by providing commands for generating components, services, modules, and more.
- **Project Structure**: Follow best practices for organizing your project into modules, components, and services based on features, and use lazy loading to optimize the app's performance.
- **Real-World Example**: We demonstrated how to build a feature-rich Angular app by creating user and auth

modules, implementing routing, and using Angular CLI to manage the app's structure.

In the next chapter, we will explore **Angular testing** and how to write unit and end-to-end tests for your Angular applications.

CHAPTER 15

VUE.JS: A LIGHTWEIGHT JAVASCRIPT FRAMEWORK

What is Vue.js and Why It's Gaining Popularity?

Vue.js is a progressive, lightweight JavaScript framework used for building user interfaces. Vue focuses on the **view layer** and can be easily integrated with other libraries or existing projects. However, it's also powerful enough to build single-page applications (SPAs) when combined with additional libraries like **Vue Router** for routing and **Vuex** for state management.

Vue.js is gaining popularity for several key reasons:

1. **Simplicity and Ease of Learning**: Vue has a gentle learning curve. It is easy for developers with basic HTML, CSS, and JavaScript knowledge to get started with. The framework is highly approachable and offers great documentation.

2. **Flexible and Modular**: Vue can be used in projects of various sizes. It can enhance the interactivity of small parts of a website, or it can be used as the core of a large single-page application (SPA).

171

3. **Reactivity System**: Vue's reactivity system makes it easy to work with dynamic data. It automatically keeps the UI in sync with the underlying data, reducing the need to manually manipulate the DOM.

4. **Lightweight**: Vue is known for being relatively small in size (compared to frameworks like Angular). This lightweight nature allows for faster initial loading times and more efficient performance.

5. **Developer Experience**: Vue provides excellent developer tools, including the Vue DevTools extension for debugging and inspecting Vue components in the browser.

6. **Community and Ecosystem**: Vue has a strong and growing community, with plenty of resources, plugins, and third-party libraries. It is also supported by tools such as Vue CLI, Vue Router, and Vuex, which help in building complex applications.

Setting Up Vue.js and Understanding Its Core Features

Setting up Vue.js is simple. Vue is designed to be incrementally adoptable, which means you can integrate it into existing projects gradually. Here are the steps to set up a basic Vue.js application:

1. **Setting Up Vue.js in a Project**:

172

o **Using a CDN**: The easiest way to start with Vue is to include it via a CDN in an HTML file. This method is best for small projects or prototypes.

html

```
<!DOCTYPE html>
<html lang="en">
    <head>
        <meta charset="UTF-8">
        <meta                name="viewport"
content="width=device-width,     initial-
scale=1.0">
        <title>Vue.js App</title>
        <script
src="https://cdn.jsdelivr.net/npm/vue@2.6
.14/dist/vue.js"></script>
    </head>
    <body>
        <div id="app">
            <h1>{{ message }}</h1>
        </div>

        <script>
            new Vue({
                el: '#app',
                data: {
                    message:        'Hello,
Vue.js!'
```

173

```
                    }
                });
            </script>
        </body>
</html>
```

In this simple example, we are linking Vue.js via CDN and creating a Vue instance that binds the `message` data property to the `<h1>` element in the HTML.

2. **Using Vue CLI for Larger Projects**: For more complex projects, it's recommended to use the Vue CLI to create and manage Vue applications. This tool helps set up development environments, manage project dependencies, and bundle assets for production.

   o First, install Vue CLI globally:

   bash

   ```
   npm install -g @vue/cli
   ```

   o Create a new Vue project:

   bash

   ```
   vue create my-vue-app
   ```

   o Follow the prompts to set up the project with default configurations or customize the setup.

Afterward, navigate into the project directory and run the development server:

```bash
cd my-vue-app
npm run serve
```

3. This will start the development server, and you can view the app in your browser at `http://localhost:8080`.

Core Features of Vue.js

1. **Reactive Data Binding**: Vue uses a reactive data-binding system that automatically updates the UI when the underlying data changes. This eliminates the need for manual DOM updates, making it easier to handle dynamic data.

```html
<div id="app">
    <input v-model="message" />
    <p>The input is: {{ message }}</p>
</div>

<script>
```

175

```
new Vue({
    el: '#app',
    data: {
        message: 'Hello, Vue!'
    }
});
</script>
```

- o **v-model**: This directive creates a two-way data binding between the input field and the `message` data property.

- o **{{ message }}**: This is Vue's interpolation syntax, which binds data to the HTML dynamically.

2. **Directives**: Vue provides several built-in directives to manage DOM elements in a declarative way. Some of the most commonly used directives include:

   - o **v-if**: Conditionally renders an element.

   - o **v-for**: Renders a list of items by iterating over an array or object.

   - o **v-bind**: Dynamically binds attributes to an element.

   - o **v-on**: Attaches event listeners to elements.

Example using `v-for` and `v-if`:

```
html
```

176

```
<ul>
    <li    v-for="item    in    items"    v-
if="item.isVisible">{{ item.name }}</li>
</ul>

<script>
    new Vue({
        el: '#app',
        data: {
            items: [
                {    name:    'Item    1',
isVisible: true },
                {    name:    'Item    2',
isVisible: false },
                {    name:    'Item    3',
isVisible: true }
            ]
        }
    });
</script>
```

In this example, `v-for` is used to loop through the `items` array, and `v-if` is used to conditionally render each item based on the `isVisible` property.

3. **Vue Components**: Vue applications are built around **components**. A component is a reusable piece of code that controls a part of the UI and has its own data, methods, and lifecycle hooks.

177

Example of a simple Vue component:

html

```html
<div id="app">
    <greeting></greeting>
</div>

<script>
    Vue.component('greeting', {
        data() {
            return {
                message: 'Hello from Vue component!'
            };
        },
        template: '<h1>{{ message }}</h1>'
    });

    new Vue({
        el: '#app'
    });
</script>
```

In this example, we define a global component named greeting that has its own message data property. The template option defines the HTML structure of the component.

Real-World Example: Building a Simple Vue.js App

Let's create a basic Vue.js application that allows users to add and remove tasks from a to-do list. This will demonstrate the use of Vue components, directives, and reactive data binding.

1. **Project Setup**: Create a new Vue project using Vue CLI as shown earlier.
2. **Create the Task List Component**:

Create a new component `TaskList.vue` to manage the list of tasks.

```vue
<template>
    <div>
        <h2>Task List</h2>
        <ul>
            <li v-for="(task, index) in tasks" :key="index">
                {{ task }}
                <button @click="removeTask(index)">Remove</button>
            </li>
        </ul>
```

179

```
        <input           v-model="newTask"
placeholder="Add a task" />
        <button          @click="addTask">Add
Task</button>
    </div>
</template>

<script>
export default {
    data() {
        return {
            tasks:    ['Buy    groceries',
'Complete Vue.js tutorial'],
            newTask: ''
        };
    },
    methods: {
        addTask() {
            if (this.newTask) {

this.tasks.push(this.newTask);
                this.newTask = '';
            }
        },
        removeTask(index) {
            this.tasks.splice(index, 1);
        }
    }
};
```

```
</script>

<style scoped>
    button {
        margin-left: 10px;
        cursor: pointer;
    }
</style>
```

In this component:

- o `tasks` is an array containing the list of tasks.
- o `newTask` is bound to the input field to allow the user to add new tasks.
- o The `addTask` method adds the task to the `tasks` array, and `removeTask` removes a task by its index.

3. **Use the Component in App.vue:**

vue

```
<template>
    <div id="app">
        <task-list></task-list>
    </div>
</template>

<script>
```

```
import            TaskList            from
'./components/TaskList.vue';

export default {
    name: 'App',
    components: {
        TaskList
    }
};
</script>

<style>
#app {
    text-align: center;
    padding: 20px;
}
</style>
```

Here, we import the `TaskList` component and use it within the `App.vue` template.

4. **Run the App**: Use the following command to start the development server:

```bash
npm run serve
```

182

You can now view the app at `http://localhost:8080/`, where you can add and remove tasks from the to-do list.

Key Takeaways:

- **Vue.js** is a lightweight and progressive JavaScript framework that focuses on the view layer and makes it easy to build interactive user interfaces.
- **Reactivity**: Vue's reactivity system simplifies working with dynamic data, automatically keeping the UI in sync with changes to the data.
- **Directives**: Vue provides several built-in directives like `v-if`, `v-for`, and `v-bind` to handle DOM manipulations and data binding in a declarative way.
- **Components**: Vue applications are built around components, which encapsulate HTML, CSS, and JavaScript logic to create reusable building blocks.
- **Real-World Example**: We built a simple to-do list app that demonstrates Vue's features, including data binding, components, and event handling.

In the next chapter, we will explore **Vue Router** and **Vuex** for managing navigation and state in larger Vue.js applications.

CHAPTER 16

VUE COMPONENTS AND VUE ROUTER

Understanding Components in Vue.js

In Vue.js, **components** are the building blocks of the user interface (UI). Each component is a reusable piece of code that encapsulates the HTML, CSS, and JavaScript logic for a part of the UI. Components can be as simple as a button or as complex as an entire page of an application.

Vue components allow you to break down your application into smaller, more manageable pieces, making it easier to develop, test, and maintain.

Key Concepts of Vue Components:

1. **Single-File Components**: Vue components are typically stored in `.vue` files, also known as Single-File Components (SFCs). These files contain three sections:
   - `<template>`: The HTML part of the component, which defines the structure of the UI.

o **<script>**: The JavaScript logic for the component, such as data, methods, computed properties, and lifecycle hooks.

o **<style>**: The CSS styling for the component, scoped to the component.

2. **Creating a Vue Component**: Components in Vue.js are easy to create. You can either define them globally or locally.

   o **Global Component**: To register a component globally, use Vue.component():

   javascript

   ```javascript
   Vue.component('my-component', {
       template: '<p>Hello, Vue!</p>'
   });
   ```

   o **Local Component**: You can also register components locally within another component:

   javascript

   ```javascript
   export default {
       components: {
           MyComponent: {
               template: '<p>Hello from MyComponent</p>'
           }
       }
   ```

185

```
};
```

3. **Props**: Components communicate with each other through **props**. A parent component can pass data to a child component using `props`:

html

```html
<child-component
:message="parentMessage"></child-
component>
```

In the child component:

javascript

```javascript
props: ['message']
```

4. **Events**: Child components can send messages to their parent using **events**. The parent listens to the event using `@event-name`:

html

```html
<button          @click="sendMessage">Send
Message</button>
```

The parent component listens for the event:

html

186

```
<child-component
@message="handleMessage"></child-
component>
```

And in the child:

```
javascript
```

```
this.$emit('message', 'Hello from Child');
```

Setting Up Vue Router for Navigation

For most modern web applications, routing is essential. **Vue Router** is the official routing library for Vue.js that allows you to handle navigation between different views or pages of your application.

Steps to Set Up Vue Router:

1. **Install Vue Router**: Vue Router is not bundled by default, so you need to install it separately:

   ```bash
   bash
   ```

   ```
   npm install vue-router
   ```

2. **Create a Router Instance**: After installing Vue Router, you need to configure it. Create a `router.js` file to define the routes:

```javascript
import Vue from 'vue';
import Router from 'vue-router';
import Home from './components/Home.vue';
import About from './components/About.vue';

Vue.use(Router);

const router = new Router({
    routes: [
        {
            path: '/',
            name: 'home',
            component: Home
        },
        {
            path: '/about',
            name: 'about',
            component: About
        }
    ]
});
```

188

```
export default router;
```

- o **path**: The URL path for the route.
- o **component**: The component to be displayed when the route is accessed.

3. **Add the Router to the Vue Instance**: Now that you've defined the routes, add the router to your Vue instance. In the main.js file, import the router and tell Vue to use it:

```javascript
import Vue from 'vue';
import App from './App.vue';
import router from './router';

new Vue({
    render: h => h(App),
    router
}).$mount('#app');
```

4. **Adding Navigation Links**: You can now use the `<router-link>` component to navigate between pages:

```html
<nav>
    <router-link to="/">Home</router-link>
    <router-link
to="/about">About</router-link>
```

189

```
</nav>
```

- o `to` is used to specify the route path.

5. **Displaying the Routed Views**: Use the `<router-view>` component to display the content based on the active route:

html

```
<div id="app">
    <router-view></router-view>
</div>
```

The `<router-view>` is where the routed components will be injected dynamically based on the URL.

Real-World Example: Building a Multi-Page Vue App with Routing

Let's create a simple multi-page Vue.js app using Vue Router. We'll create two pages: **Home** and **About**.

1. **Set Up the Project**: If you haven't already, create a new Vue project using Vue CLI:

bash

```
vue create vue-router-example
```

2. **Install Vue Router**: Install Vue Router in your project:

```bash
npm install vue-router
```

3. **Create Components**: In the `src/components` directory, create two components: `Home.vue` and `About.vue`.

Home.vue:

```vue
<template>
    <div>
        <h1>Welcome to the Home Page</h1>
        <p>This is the home page of our app.</p>
    </div>
</template>

<script>
export default {
    name: 'Home'
};
</script>
```

191

About.vue:

```vue
<template>
    <div>
        <h1>About Us</h1>
        <p>This page provides information
about the app.</p>
    </div>
</template>

<script>
export default {
    name: 'About'
};
</script>
```

4. **Create Router Configuration**: In `src/router/index.js`, configure Vue Router and set up the routes:

```javascript
import Vue from 'vue';
import Router from 'vue-router';
import Home from '@/components/Home.vue';
import About from
'@/components/About.vue';
```

```
Vue.use(Router);

export default new Router({
    routes: [
        {
            path: '/',
            name: 'Home',
            component: Home
        },
        {
            path: '/about',
            name: 'About',
            component: About
        }
    ]
});
```

5. **Add Router to the Vue Instance**: In src/main.js, import and use the router:

```javascript
javascript

import Vue from 'vue';
import App from './App.vue';
import router from './router';

Vue.config.productionTip = false;

new Vue({
    render: h => h(App),
```

193

```
    router
}).$mount('#app');
```

6. **Add Navigation Links**: In `src/App.vue`, add navigation links using `router-link` and display the views using `router-view`:

```vue
vue

<template>
    <div id="app">
        <nav>
            <router-link
to="/">Home</router-link> |
            <router-link
to="/about">About</router-link>
        </nav>
        <router-view></router-view>
    </div>
</template>

<script>
export default {
    name: 'App'
};
</script>
```

7. **Run the Application**: Now, run the application using the Vue CLI's development server:

```bash
bash

npm run serve
```

Navigate to `http://localhost:8080/`, and you should see the home page. By clicking on the **About** link in the navigation bar, you'll be navigated to the **About** page, with the content of the page changing dynamically based on the route.

Key Takeaways:

- **Vue Components**: Components in Vue are reusable building blocks of the application, defined using the `<template>`, `<script>`, and `<style>` sections.
- **Vue Router**: Vue Router allows you to navigate between different pages of your app without reloading the page, enabling single-page applications (SPA).
- **Setting Up Routing**: By creating a `router.js` file, you can define the routes and associate them with components, and use `<router-link>` and `<router-view>` for navigation.
- **Real-World Example**: We built a multi-page Vue app with a Home and About page, utilizing Vue Router for navigation and dynamic content rendering.

195

In the next chapter, we will explore **Vuex** for managing application state in large-scale Vue applications, allowing for more centralized and scalable state management.

CHAPTER 17

STATE MANAGEMENT IN VUE WITH VUEX

What is Vuex and Why Is It Used for State Management?

In modern web applications, managing state can become complex, especially when data needs to be shared between multiple components. **Vuex** is a state management library for **Vue.js** that provides a centralized store to manage application state in a predictable way.

Vuex is used primarily to handle **shared state** (data that is needed by multiple components) and provides a centralized mechanism for updating and accessing that state. It ensures that components do not have to rely on passing data up and down the component hierarchy via props and events, which can become unwieldy in large applications.

Why Use Vuex?

- **Centralized State**: Vuex provides a single source of truth for your application's state. All state is stored in one place, which makes it easier to track and manage.

- **Predictable State Changes**: Vuex enforces strict rules on how state is mutated, which leads to predictable and traceable changes.
- **Integration with Vue's Reactivity System**: Vuex seamlessly integrates with Vue's reactivity system, ensuring that state changes automatically trigger UI updates.
- **Handling Complex State**: For large applications with complex state management needs, Vuex simplifies managing state across multiple components, improving maintainability and scalability.

Setting Up Vuex in a Vue App

Setting up Vuex in your Vue.js application is straightforward. Here are the steps to get started:

1. **Install Vuex**: First, you need to install Vuex. If you're using Vue CLI, Vuex can be installed with the following command:

```bash
npm install vuex
```

2. **Create a Vuex Store**: In Vue, the **store** is where all the application state is kept. The store in Vuex contains **state**, **mutations**, **actions**, and **getters**:

   o **State**: Holds the application's data.

   o **Mutations**: Synchronous methods that change the state.

   o **Actions**: Asynchronous methods that can commit mutations.

   o **Getters**: Methods for retrieving state in a computed-like manner.

You can create a Vuex store by creating a file, store.js, and setting up the store:

```javascript
import Vue from 'vue';
import Vuex from 'vuex';

Vue.use(Vuex);

export default new Vuex.Store({
    state: {
        count: 0
    },
    mutations: {
        increment(state) {
            state.count++;
```

```
        },
        decrement(state) {
            state.count--;
        }
    },
    actions: {
        incrementAsync({ commit }) {
            setTimeout(() => {
                commit('increment');
            }, 1000);
        }
    },
    getters: {
        currentCount: state => state.count
    }
});
```

In this store:

- o **State**: The `count` property holds the current count.
- o **Mutations**: `increment` and `decrement` mutate the state.
- o **Actions**: `incrementAsync` is an asynchronous action that commits the `increment` mutation after a delay.
- o **Getters**: `currentCount` is a getter to access the current count from the state.

3. **Integrating Vuex Store into Vue App**: Once the store is created, you need to integrate it into your Vue app. In `main.js`, import the store and pass it to the Vue instance:

```javascript
import Vue from 'vue';
import App from './App.vue';
import store from './store';

Vue.config.productionTip = false;

new Vue({
    render: h => h(App),
    store
}).$mount('#app');
```

This allows the Vuex store to be available in all components via the `this.$store` property.

Real-World Example: Managing App State with Vuex in a Shopping App

Let's build a simple shopping app where we manage the state of a shopping cart using Vuex. We will have the following features:

• Add items to the cart.

- Remove items from the cart.
- View the total number of items in the cart.

1. **Set Up Vuex Store**: First, create a Vuex store that will manage the state of the shopping cart. The store will contain:
    - **State**: The list of items in the cart and the total number of items.
    - **Mutations**: Methods for adding and removing items from the cart.
    - **Actions**: Asynchronous actions to simulate fetching items (e.g., adding a new item).
    - **Getters**: To calculate the total number of items and total price.

store.js:

```javascript
import Vue from 'vue';
import Vuex from 'vuex';

Vue.use(Vuex);

export default new Vuex.Store({
    state: {
        cart: []
    },
```

```
mutations: {
    addItem(state, item) {
        state.cart.push(item);
    },
    removeItem(state, itemIndex) {
        state.cart.splice(itemIndex,
1);
    }
},
actions: {
    addItemAsync({ commit }, item) {
        setTimeout(() => {
            commit('addItem', item);
        }, 1000);
    }
},
getters: {
    cartItemCount(state) {
        return state.cart.length;
    },
    cartTotalPrice(state) {
        return
state.cart.reduce((total, item) => total +
item.price, 0);
    }
}
});
```

In this store:

- o **State**: The `cart` holds the list of items in the cart.
- o **Mutations**: `addItem` and `removeItem` are used to add and remove items from the cart.
- o **Actions**: `addItemAsync` simulates an asynchronous action to add an item to the cart after a delay.
- o **Getters**: `cartItemCount` returns the number of items in the cart, and `cartTotalPrice` calculates the total price of the items.

2. **Create Components**: Now, let's create components for the shopping cart and the item list.

App.vue:

vue

```
<template>
    <div id="app">
        <h1>Shopping Cart</h1>
        <item-list></item-list>
        <cart-summary></cart-summary>
    </div>
</template>

<script>
import          ItemList          from
'./components/ItemList.vue';
```

```
import          CartSummary          from
'./components/CartSummary.vue';

export default {
    name: 'App',
    components: {
        ItemList,
        CartSummary
    }
};
</script>
```

ItemList.vue:

vue

```
<template>
    <div>
        <h2>Items for Sale</h2>
        <ul>
            <li  v-for="(item,  index)  in
items" :key="index">
                {{  item.name  }}  -  ${{
item.price }}
                <button
@click="addItemToCart(item)">Add          to
Cart</button>
            </li>
        </ul>
    </div>
```

```
</template>

<script>
export default {
    data() {
        return {
            items: [
                { name: 'Apple', price: 1
},
                { name: 'Banana', price:
0.5 },
                { name: 'Orange', price:
0.8 }
            ]
        };
    },
    methods: {
        addItemToCart(item) {

this.$store.dispatch('addItemAsync',
item);
        }
    }
};
</script>
```

In this component:

- o We define a list of items available for sale.

o The `addItemToCart` method dispatches the `addItemAsync` action to add the selected item to the cart.

CartSummary.vue:

vue

```
<template>
    <div>
        <h2>Cart Summary</h2>
        <p>Total Items: {{ cartItemCount
}}</p>
        <p>Total Price: ${{ cartTotalPrice
}}</p>
        <button  @click="clearCart">Clear
Cart</button>
    </div>
</template>

<script>
export default {
    computed: {
        cartItemCount() {
            return
this.$store.getters.cartItemCount;
        },
        cartTotalPrice() {
```

```
        return
this.$store.getters.cartTotalPrice;
        }
    },
    methods: {
        clearCart() {
            this.$store.state.cart = [];
        }
    }
};
</script>
```

In this component:

- o We use Vuex **getters** to display the total number of items and the total price of the cart.
- o The `clearCart` method resets the cart by directly modifying the `cart` state.

3. **Run the App**: Now, start the Vue development server:

```bash
bash
```

```
npm run serve
```

Visit `http://localhost:8080/` to see the shopping cart in action. You can add items to the cart, view the total number of items and price, and clear the cart.

Key Takeaways:

- **Vuex**: Vuex is a state management pattern and library for managing the application's state in a centralized store. It is useful for handling shared state across multiple components, especially in large applications.

- **State, Mutations, Actions, and Getters**: Vuex uses state to hold data, mutations to change state, actions for asynchronous operations, and getters for accessing and computing state.

- **Real-World Example**: We created a shopping app with Vuex to manage the shopping cart state. We used Vuex to handle adding/removing items and calculating the total price, demonstrating how Vuex can help manage state in complex applications.

In the next chapter, we will explore **Vuex Modules** for better organizing state management in large Vue applications.

CHAPTER 18

COMPARING REACT, ANGULAR, AND VUE.JS

Key Differences Between React, Angular, and Vue.js

React, Angular, and Vue.js are three of the most popular JavaScript frameworks/libraries for building modern web applications. While they all serve a similar purpose—helping developers create dynamic, interactive user interfaces—they differ in their architecture, complexity, and philosophy. Understanding these differences will help you choose the right tool for your project based on your specific requirements.

React: A JavaScript Library for Building UI Components

- **Core Philosophy**: React is a **library**, not a full-fledged framework. Its primary goal is to build UI components and handle the view layer in applications. It is unopinionated, allowing you to integrate it with other libraries for routing, state management, and other functionalities.

- **Component-Based Architecture**: React apps are built around reusable components. Each component can have its own state and logic, and components are composed together to create the user interface.

- **One-Way Data Flow**: React uses one-way data binding, meaning data flows from parent components to child components through props. This makes React predictable and easy to debug.

- **JSX (JavaScript XML)**: React components are written using JSX, which is a syntax extension that looks similar to HTML but allows you to embed JavaScript logic inside the markup.

- **Ecosystem**: React's ecosystem is extensive but modular. You are free to pick libraries for routing (React Router), state management (Redux, Context API), and other features.

- **Learning Curve**: React has a relatively low learning curve compared to Angular. The main challenge is understanding how to integrate React with other tools and manage state in larger applications.

Angular: A Full-Featured Framework

- **Core Philosophy**: Angular is a **full-fledged framework** that provides everything you need to build complex web

211

applications, including routing, forms management, HTTP requests, and state management.

- **Component-Based Architecture**: Like React, Angular uses a component-based architecture, but components in Angular are more complex and come with built-in features like dependency injection, lifecycle hooks, and directives.

- **Two-Way Data Binding**: Angular uses two-way data binding, where changes to the model automatically update the view and vice versa. This is convenient for forms and user input but can lead to performance issues in large applications.

- **TypeScript**: Angular is built with **TypeScript**, a superset of JavaScript that provides static typing. While TypeScript adds additional complexity, it also helps with maintainability and catching errors early in the development process.

- **Built-in Features**: Angular comes with built-in tools for routing, state management, forms, and HTTP requests, making it a complete solution for building enterprise-grade applications.

- **Learning Curve**: Angular has a steep learning curve due to its extensive feature set and reliance on TypeScript. Developers need to understand concepts like decorators, dependency injection, and RxJS to effectively work with Angular.

212

Vue.js: A Progressive Framework

- **Core Philosophy**: Vue.js is a **progressive framework** designed to be incrementally adoptable. It's lightweight and flexible, making it suitable for both small and large-scale applications. Vue is designed to be simple and approachable while providing advanced features for complex use cases.

- **Component-Based Architecture**: Like React and Angular, Vue.js uses a component-based architecture. Vue components are easy to create and are defined in single-file `.vue` files, which encapsulate the template, script, and styles for a component.

- **Two-Way Data Binding**: Vue provides two-way data binding, similar to Angular. This is achieved using the `v-model` directive, which makes it easy to handle form inputs and synchronize data between the model and the view.

- **Flexibility**: Vue allows you to scale your application gradually. You can use Vue to enhance small parts of an application or as a full framework for building large applications. Vue can also be integrated with other libraries or existing projects easily.

- **Learning Curve**: Vue has one of the easiest learning curves among the three. It is designed to be simple and intuitive, with great documentation and a gentle introduction to concepts like directives, components, and state management.

Comparing React, Angular, and Vue.js

Feature	React	Angular	Vue.js
Type	Library	Full-Featured Framework	Progressive Framework
Core Focus	UI Components	Full Web Application Development	Flexible, UI Development
Data Binding	One-Way Data Flow	Two-Way Data Binding	Two-Way Data Binding
State Management	Unopinionated (Redux, Context API)	Built-in (Services, RxJS)	Built-in (Vuex)
Language	JavaScript (JSX)	TypeScript	JavaScript (with optional TypeScript)

214

Feature	React	Angular	Vue.js
Learning Curve	Easy for beginners, harder for large apps	Steep learning curve due to TypeScript and RxJS	Easy to learn, especially for small to medium projects
Performance	High, due to virtual DOM	High, but two-way binding may cause performance issues	High, thanks to efficient reactivity system
Routing	React Router	Built-in Router	Vue Router
Ecosystem	Modular (React Router, Redux)	All-in-one (routing, state management, etc.)	Modular and flexible (Vuex, Vue Router)

Which Framework is Best for Your Project Based on Requirements?

215

The choice between React, Angular, and Vue depends on your project's specific requirements. Below are some guidelines for selecting the right framework:

Use React If:

- You need a **library** for building dynamic UIs and prefer flexibility in choosing your tools.
- Your app is relatively simple or you want to incrementally add features to an existing project.
- You are building a single-page application (SPA) and need a lightweight, fast solution.
- You prefer working with JavaScript (and JSX), and you have experience with modern JavaScript features.

Use Angular If:

- You are building a **large-scale, enterprise-level** application that needs an all-in-one solution with built-in features like routing, forms, and HTTP services.
- You prefer **TypeScript** and need strong typing and static analysis for maintainability.
- You need to work with complex architectures and handle more advanced topics like dependency injection and RxJS.

Use Vue.js If:

- You need a **flexible, progressive** framework that can be used for both small and large applications.

- You want something that is easy to learn, especially if you're new to JavaScript frameworks.

- You are working on a **project that requires gradual adoption**, such as integrating Vue into an existing app.

- You prefer **simplicity** but still need the power of an advanced state management solution (Vuex) and router (Vue Router) for larger projects.

Real-World Example: Comparing App Performance Across These Frameworks

To understand the performance differences, let's consider building a **To-Do List Application** in React, Angular, and Vue.js. We will measure the following aspects of performance:

1. **Initial Load Time**: How quickly does the application load and render the UI for the first time?

2. **Update Performance**: How quickly does the application update the UI when a user adds, edits, or removes a to-do item?

3. **Memory Usage**: How much memory does the application consume as the list grows?

Performance Testing Setup:

1. **React**: Create a simple To-Do app using `useState` for state management and `map` to render the list.
2. **Angular**: Create a To-Do app using Angular components and services for state management.
3. **Vue.js**: Create a Vue To-Do app using `data` for state management and `v-for` to render the list.

After building the three apps, use tools like **Lighthouse** in Chrome DevTools or **WebPageTest** to analyze the following:

- **Time to First Byte** (TTFB) and **First Contentful Paint** (FCP) for initial load time.
- **Time to Interactive** (TTI) for responsiveness.
- **Memory footprint** using browser memory analysis tools.

Expected Results:

- **React**: Due to its virtual DOM and efficient diffing algorithm, React usually performs very well for both updates and rendering, especially for dynamic content.
- **Angular**: While Angular's two-way data binding can make it more resource-intensive, its performance is generally strong when optimized (e.g., using `OnPush` change detection strategy).
- **Vue.js**: Vue's reactive system ensures high performance, and it typically performs as well as React in terms of rendering and updates.

Key Takeaways:

- **React**: Ideal for dynamic UI components with flexibility and a focus on the view layer. It's great for SPAs and projects where you need control over state management.
- **Angular**: A complete framework, best suited for large-scale applications that need built-in routing, forms, and services. Its use of TypeScript and advanced features like RxJS provides scalability but comes with a steeper learning curve.
- **Vue.js**: A progressive framework that is easy to learn and can be scaled for larger projects with Vuex and Vue Router. It's perfect for both small enhancements and full-fledged applications, providing flexibility and simplicity.

In the next chapter, we will explore **Testing** in React, Angular, and Vue.js, comparing tools and best practices for ensuring your application's quality through automated tests.

CHAPTER 19

BUILDING A FULL-STACK APP WITH REACT

Understanding the Full-Stack Development Approach

In a full-stack application, the term "stack" refers to the combination of technologies used for both the **front-end** and **back-end** of the application. A full-stack app typically consists of:

- **Front-End**: The client-side of the app, responsible for the user interface (UI). It is often built using JavaScript frameworks like React, Angular, or Vue.js.
- **Back-End**: The server-side of the app, responsible for handling requests, managing databases, and serving data to the front-end. Common back-end technologies include Node.js, Express, and databases like MongoDB or SQL.

Building a full-stack app means integrating both the front-end and back-end, allowing them to communicate with each other. The front-end sends requests to the back-end, which processes the requests, interacts with the database, and sends back a response that the front-end can display.

Setting Up a Back-End (Node.js + Express) with React

To build a full-stack app using React for the front-end and Node.js/Express for the back-end, we need to follow these steps:

1. Setting Up the Back-End with Node.js and Express

Start by setting up the back-end to handle HTTP requests and interact with a database. We will use **Node.js** for the runtime environment and **Express** to create the REST API.

1. **Initialize a New Node.js Project**: Create a directory for your back-end, navigate to it, and run `npm init` to set up your project:

   bash

   ```
   mkdir backend
   cd backend
   npm init -y
   ```

2. **Install Dependencies**: Install the required packages for the back-end, including **Express** (for building the API) and **cors** (for enabling cross-origin requests from the React front-end):

```bash
npm install express cors
```

3. **Set Up Express Server**: Create a file named `server.js` in the `backend` directory. This will set up the Express server to listen for incoming requests:

```javascript
const express = require('express');
const cors = require('cors');

const app = express();
const port = 5000;

// Middleware
app.use(cors());
app.use(express.json()); // To parse JSON bodies

// Routes
app.get('/', (req, res) => {
    res.send('Hello from the back-end!');
});

// Start the server
app.listen(port, () => {
```

```
        console.log(`Server   is   running   on
http://localhost:${port}`);
});
```

4. **Start the Express Server**: Run the server with Node.js:

```bash

node server.js
```

The back-end server should now be running at `http://localhost:5000`.

2. Setting Up the Front-End with React

Next, we will set up the React front-end to interact with the back-end.

1. **Create a React Project**: Use the **Create React App** tool to set up the front-end:

```bash

npx create-react-app frontend
cd frontend
```

2. **Install Axios for HTTP Requests**: Install **Axios**, a popular library for making HTTP requests from the React app to the Express server:

223

```bash
npm install axios
```

3. **Create a Component to Fetch Data**: In the `src` directory of the React app, create a new file called `App.js` (if it doesn't already exist). Modify it to make an HTTP request to the back-end:

```javascript
import React, { useEffect, useState } from 'react';
import axios from 'axios';

const App = () => {
    const [message, setMessage] = useState('');

    useEffect(() => {
        // Fetch data from the back-end

axios.get('http://localhost:5000')
            .then(response => {

setMessage(response.data);
            })
            .catch(error => {
```

```
            console.error('There    was
an error fetching the data!', error);
        });
    }, []);

    return (
        <div>
            <h1>{message}</h1>
        </div>
    );
};

export default App;
```

In this example, **Axios** makes a GET request to the back-end at `http://localhost:5000`. The response from the server is stored in the `message` state, which is then displayed in the UI.

4. **Start the React App**: Run the React app using the following command:

```bash
npm start
```

The front-end should now be running at `http://localhost:3000` and should display the message received from the back-end.

225

Real-World Example: Building a Full-Stack App with React and Express

Let's extend this setup to build a full-stack to-do list app, where users can add tasks to a to-do list, save them to the back-end, and display them on the front-end.

1. Back-End (Node.js + Express)

1. **Create the To-Do Routes**: In the `server.js` file, create routes for adding and fetching tasks. You can use an in-memory array for storing tasks temporarily.

   javascript

   ```javascript
   const express = require('express');
   const cors = require('cors');

   const app = express();
   const port = 5000;

   app.use(cors());
   app.use(express.json());

   let tasks = [];  // In-memory storage for
   tasks
   ```

```
// Get all tasks
app.get('/tasks', (req, res) => {
    res.json(tasks);
});

// Add a task
app.post('/tasks', (req, res) => {
    const { task } = req.body;
    tasks.push({ id: tasks.length + 1, task
});
    res.status(201).json({ message: 'Task
added successfully' });
});

// Start the server
app.listen(port, () => {
    console.log(`Server   is   running   on
http://localhost:${port}`);
});
```

2. **Testing the Back-End**: The `/tasks` endpoint will return all tasks, and the `/tasks POST` endpoint will allow adding new tasks.

2. Front-End (React)

1. **Fetching Tasks in React**: Modify the `App.js` component to fetch tasks from the back-end and display them.

227

```javascript
javascript

import React, { useState, useEffect } from
'react';
import axios from 'axios';

const App = () => {
    const    [tasks,    setTasks]    =
useState([]);
    const    [newTask,    setNewTask]    =
useState('');

    useEffect(() => {
        // Fetch tasks from the back-end

axios.get('http://localhost:5000/tasks')
            .then(response => {
                setTasks(response.data);
            })
            .catch(error => {
                console.error('Error
fetching tasks:', error);
            });
    }, []);

    const handleAddTask = () => {
        if (newTask) {
```

```javascript
axios.post('http://localhost:5000/tasks',
{ task: newTask })
            .then(response => {
                setTasks([...tasks,  {
id: tasks.length + 1, task: newTask }]);
                setNewTask('');
            })
            .catch(error => {
                console.error('Error
adding task:', error);
            });
    }
  };

  return (
    <div>
        <h1>To-Do List</h1>
        <input
            type="text"
            value={newTask}
            onChange={(e)            =>
setNewTask(e.target.value)}
            placeholder="Add    a    new
task"
        />
        <button
onClick={handleAddTask}>Add Task</button>
        <ul>
```

229

```
{tasks.map((task) => (
    <li
key={task.id}>{task.task}</li>
        ))}
    </ul>
  </div>
 );
};

export default App;
```

In this example:

- ○ **GET /tasks** is used to fetch the list of tasks from the back-end.
- ○ **POST /tasks** is used to add a new task to the back-end. The new task is then added to the state and displayed in the UI.

2. **Styling and Final Touches**: You can enhance the UI with additional features like deleting tasks or marking them as completed. Add CSS for styling and provide user feedback, such as success or error messages when adding tasks.

3. Running the Full-Stack App

1. **Start the Back-End**: In the `backend` folder, run the server:

```
bash
```

```
node server.js
```

2. **Start the Front-End**: In the `frontend` folder, run the React app:

```
bash
```

```
npm start
```

Your full-stack app is now up and running! The front-end (React) communicates with the back-end (Node.js/Express) to manage tasks, and all the data is persisted on the server.

Key Takeaways:

- **Full-Stack Development**: Building a full-stack app involves combining the front-end (React) with the back-end (Node.js/Express) to create a complete solution where the front-end and back-end communicate with each other.
- **Node.js + Express**: This back-end setup allows you to create RESTful APIs, handle HTTP requests, and manage application data.

- **React**: The front-end is built with React, which communicates with the back-end via HTTP requests (using Axios) to fetch and submit data.
- **Real-World Example**: We built a to-do list app where tasks are added and fetched from the back-end, demonstrating the integration between React and Express in a full-stack application.

In the next chapter, we will explore **Deploying Full-Stack Apps**, covering how to deploy both the front-end and back-end parts of the application to production environments.

232

CHAPTER 20

BUILDING A FULL-STACK APP WITH ANGULAR

Setting Up an Angular Front-End with a Node.js Back-End

Building a full-stack application with **Angular** for the front-end and **Node.js** for the back-end allows you to create a powerful and scalable web application. In this chapter, we'll walk through the steps to set up a complete full-stack Angular app that interacts with a Node.js server. We will focus on creating an API in **Node.js/Express** and connecting it to an **Angular** app to handle CRUD operations (Create, Read, Update, and Delete).

Step 1: Setting Up the Node.js Back-End

1. **Initialize the Node.js Project**: First, set up the back-end by initializing a new Node.js project. Open a terminal and create a new directory for your back-end.

   bash

   ```
   mkdir backend
   cd backend
   ```

```
npm init -y
```

This command generates a `package.json` file.

2. **Install Dependencies**: You'll need **Express** to create a server and **cors** to handle cross-origin requests from the Angular front-end.

```bash
npm install express cors
```

3. **Create the Express Server**: Create a `server.js` file that sets up an Express server to handle API requests.

```javascript
const express = require('express');
const cors = require('cors');
const app = express();
const port = 5000;

// Middleware
app.use(cors());
app.use(express.json()); // To parse JSON
bodies

// Sample data
let users = [
```

```javascript
    { id: 1, name: 'John Doe', email:
'john.doe@example.com' },
    { id: 2, name: 'Jane Doe', email:
'jane.doe@example.com' }
];

// GET route to fetch all users
app.get('/users', (req, res) => {
    res.json(users);
});

// POST route to add a new user
app.post('/users', (req, res) => {
    const newUser = req.body;
    newUser.id = users.length + 1;
    users.push(newUser);
    res.status(201).json(newUser);
});

// PUT route to update user details
app.put('/users/:id', (req, res) => {
    const { id } = req.params;
    const updatedUser = req.body;
    users = users.map(user =>
        user.id === parseInt(id) ? {
...user, ...updatedUser } : user
    );
    res.json(updatedUser);
});
```

235

```
// DELETE route to remove a user
app.delete('/users/:id', (req, res) => {
    const { id } = req.params;
    users = users.filter(user => user.id
!== parseInt(id));
    res.status(204).send();
});


// Start the server
app.listen(port, () => {
    console.log(`Server       running       on
http://localhost:${port}`);
});
```

This back-end is set up with basic routes for handling CRUD operations on a `users` resource:

- o `GET /users`: Fetches the list of users.
- o `POST /users`: Adds a new user to the list.
- o `PUT /users/:id`: Updates an existing user's information.
- o `DELETE /users/:id`: Removes a user from the list.

4. **Start the Server**: To run the server, use:

```bash

node server.js
```

The   server   will   be   available   at
`http://localhost:5000.`

Step 2: Setting Up the Angular Front-End

1. **Create an Angular Project**: Now, let's set up the Angular front-end. Open a terminal and create a new Angular project.

```bash
```

```
ng new frontend
cd frontend
```

Choose `No` for routing when prompted and select your preferred stylesheet format (CSS, SCSS, etc.).

2. **Install HTTP Client Module**: Angular's HTTP client module allows us to send HTTP requests to the back-end. Make sure to import it in the `app.module.ts` file.

Open `src/app/app.module.ts` and add the following import:

```typescript
```

237

```
import    {    HttpClientModule    }    from
'@angular/common/http';
```

Then, include it in the imports array:

```
typescript
```

```
@NgModule({
  declarations: [AppComponent],
  imports:                   [BrowserModule,
HttpClientModule],
  providers: [],
  bootstrap: [AppComponent]
})
export class AppModule {}
```

3. **Creating the Service to Handle API Calls**: Create a service to handle the interaction with the back-end API. Run the following command to generate a service:

```
bash
```

```
ng generate service user
```

In the generated user.service.ts, set up methods for fetching, adding, updating, and deleting users.

```
typescript
```

```
import { Injectable } from '@angular/core';
```

```typescript
import { HttpClient } from
'@angular/common/http';
import { Observable } from 'rxjs';

@Injectable({
  providedIn: 'root'
})
export class UserService {
  private apiUrl =
'http://localhost:5000/users';

  constructor(private http: HttpClient) {}

  getUsers(): Observable<any> {
    return this.http.get(this.apiUrl);
  }

  addUser(user: any): Observable<any> {
    return this.http.post(this.apiUrl,
user);
  }

  updateUser(id: number, user: any):
Observable<any> {
    return
this.http.put(`${this.apiUrl}/${id}`,
user);
  }
```

```
deleteUser(id: number): Observable<any>
{
    return
this.http.delete(`${this.apiUrl}/${id}`);
  }
}
```

4. **Create Components for Displaying and Managing Users**: Now, generate components for listing users and adding/editing user details:

bash

```
ng generate component user-list
ng generate component user-form
```

user-list.component.ts: This component will display the list of users fetched from the back-end.

typescript

```
import { Component, OnInit } from
'@angular/core';
import { UserService } from
'../user.service';

@Component({
  selector: 'app-user-list',
  templateUrl:                     './user-
list.component.html',
```

```
  styleUrls: ['./user-list.component.css']
})
export class UserListComponent implements
OnInit {
  users: any[] = [];

  constructor(private       userService:
UserService) {}

  ngOnInit() {

this.userService.getUsers().subscribe(dat
a => {
      this.users = data;
    });
  }

  deleteUser(id: number) {

this.userService.deleteUser(id).subscribe
(() => {
      this.users = this.users.filter(user
=> user.id !== id);
    });
  }
}
```

user-list.component.html:

```
html
```

```
<h1>Users</h1>
<ul>
  <li *ngFor="let user of users">
    {{ user.name }} - {{ user.email }}
    <button
(click)="deleteUser(user.id)">Delete</but
ton>
  </li>
</ul>
```

user-form.component.ts: This component will allow users to add or edit user details.

```
typescript

import { Component, OnInit } from
'@angular/core';
import { UserService } from
'../user.service';
import { Router } from '@angular/router';

@Component({
  selector: 'app-user-form',
  templateUrl:                  './user-
form.component.html',
  styleUrls: ['./user-form.component.css']
})
export class UserFormComponent implements
OnInit {
```

```
user = { name: '', email: '' };

constructor(private          userService:
UserService, private router: Router) {}

ngOnInit(): void {}

onSubmit() {

this.userService.addUser(this.user).subsc
ribe(() => {
    this.router.navigate(['/users']);
  });
  }
}
```

user-form.component.html:

```
html

<h1>Add New User</h1>
<form (ngSubmit)="onSubmit()">
  <label for="name">Name:</label>
  <input id="name" [(ngModel)]="user.name"
name="name" required />

  <label for="email">Email:</label>
  <input                      id="email"
[(ngModel)]="user.email"      name="email"
required />
```

```
<button type="submit">Submit</button>
</form>
```

5. **Set Up Routing**: Set up routing to navigate between the user list and the user form. Open `src/app/app-routing.module.ts` and define routes:

typescript

```typescript
import { NgModule } from '@angular/core';
import { RouterModule, Routes } from '@angular/router';
import { UserListComponent } from './user-list/user-list.component';
import { UserFormComponent } from './user-form/user-form.component';

const routes: Routes = [
    { path: 'users', component: UserListComponent },
    { path: 'add-user', component: UserFormComponent },
    { path: '', redirectTo: '/users', pathMatch: 'full' }
];

@NgModule({
  imports: [RouterModule.forRoot(routes)],
```

```
    exports: [RouterModule]
})
export class AppRoutingModule {}
```

In `app.component.html`, add links for navigation:

```html
html
```

```html
<nav>
  <a routerLink="/users">User List</a> |
  <a routerLink="/add-user">Add User</a>
</nav>
<router-outlet></router-outlet>
```

Real-World Example: Building a Full-Stack App with Angular and Node.js

In this real-world example:

- The **back-end** is built with Node.js and Express, providing a REST API for managing users.
- The **front-end** is built with Angular, using HTTP client services to fetch, add, update, and delete users from the server.
- The app has features like viewing a list of users, adding new users, and deleting users, and it's connected to the back-end via API calls.

To run the full-stack app:

1. Start the back-end server (`node server.js` in the `backend` folder).

2. Start the Angular front-end (`npm start` in the `frontend` folder).

The full-stack app allows users to interact with both the front-end and back-end seamlessly.

Key Takeaways:

- **Node.js + Express**: Used for building the back-end API that handles data processing and serves data to the front-end.

- **Angular**: Used to build the front-end, with HTTP client services to make API calls and display data from the back-end.

- **Full-Stack Integration**: Reacting to user inputs in Angular and sending HTTP requests to Node.js for CRUD operations demonstrates the power of full-stack applications.

In the next chapter, we will explore **Deploying Full-Stack Apps** to production environments, covering how to deploy both the front-end and back-end to platforms like Heroku, AWS, and DigitalOcean.

CHAPTER 21

TESTING IN REACT

Understanding Unit Testing and Integration Testing

In software development, **testing** plays a crucial role in ensuring the correctness and reliability of your code. React, being a popular JavaScript library for building user interfaces, provides tools and techniques to make testing easier and more efficient.

Testing can be categorized into two main types:

1. Unit Testing

- **Definition**: Unit testing focuses on testing individual components or functions in isolation, ensuring that they work as expected.
- **Purpose**: The goal of unit testing is to verify the correctness of the smallest units of your application, such as individual functions or methods, without dependencies or interactions with other parts of the app.
- **Example**: Testing a function that calculates the total price of items in a shopping cart.

2. Integration Testing

- **Definition**: Integration testing checks how multiple units or components work together when integrated. This can include testing interactions between components, modules, or even external systems (e.g., APIs).

- **Purpose**: Integration testing ensures that the various pieces of your application work as expected when combined. It simulates real-world scenarios where multiple components interact.

- **Example**: Testing the interaction between a form component and a submit button, ensuring that the form submits the data correctly to the back-end.

In this chapter, we'll primarily focus on **unit testing React components** and briefly touch on **integration testing**.

Using Jest and React Testing Library for Testing React Components

To test React components, we commonly use two libraries:

1. **Jest**: A testing framework that provides utilities to run tests, mock functions, and handle assertions.

2. **React Testing Library**: A library that helps us test React components in a way that focuses on how users interact with the application rather than how the components are implemented.

1. Jest

Jest is a testing framework developed by Facebook. It works well with React and provides a rich set of features like:

- **Assertions**: Methods to test expected outcomes (e.g., `expect(value).toBe(true)`).
- **Mocking**: Allows you to mock functions, modules, and timers.
- **Spying**: Let's you track how functions are called.

Installation: If you created your React app using Create React App, Jest is already set up. If not, you can install Jest using npm:

```bash

npm install --save-dev jest
```

You can then run tests using:

```bash

npm test
```

2. React Testing Library

React Testing Library provides utility functions to simulate real-world user interactions with your React components. It encourages you to test components based on their behavior and how users would interact with them rather than focusing on implementation details (like testing internal state).

Installation: You can install React Testing Library by running:

```bash
```

```
npm install --save-dev @testing-library/react
@testing-library/jest-dom
```

- **@testing-library/react**: Provides functions to render React components and interact with them in tests.
- **@testing-library/jest-dom**: Extends Jest with custom matchers for DOM elements, such as .toBeInTheDocument().

Basic Setup Example:

A typical test file looks like this:

```javascript
```

```
import { render, screen, fireEvent } from
'@testing-library/react';
import '@testing-library/jest-dom'; // For
custom matchers like .toBeInTheDocument
import MyComponent from './MyComponent';
```

```
test('renders the component and interacts with
it', () => {
  render(<MyComponent />);

  // Find an element
  const button = screen.getByText('Click Me');
  expect(button).toBeInTheDocument();

  // Simulate user interaction
  fireEvent.click(button);

  // Test if the interaction had the expected
outcome
  expect(screen.getByText('Button
clicked')).toBeInTheDocument();
});
```

In this test:

- `render(<MyComponent />)` renders the component into the virtual DOM.
- `screen.getByText('Click Me')` finds an element by its text content.
- `fireEvent.click(button)` simulates a user clicking the button.
- `expect(screen.getByText('Button clicked'))` checks if the text "Button clicked" appears after the click event.

Real-World Example: Writing Tests for React Components

Let's now walk through a **real-world example** of writing tests for a simple React component.

Example: ToDo App Component

Suppose you have a ToDo component that allows users to add a to-do item to a list. It consists of:

1. An input field to type a task.
2. A button to add the task to the list.
3. A list of tasks that get displayed below the input.

ToDo Component (ToDo.js):

```javascript
import React, { useState } from 'react';

const ToDo = () => {
  const [task, setTask] = useState('');
  const [tasks, setTasks] = useState([]);

  const handleInputChange = (e) => {
    setTask(e.target.value);
  };
```

```
const handleAddTask = () => {
  if (task) {
    setTasks([...tasks, task]);
    setTask('');
  }
};

return (
  <div>
    <input
      type="text"
      value={task}
      onChange={handleInputChange}
      placeholder="Add a task"
    />
    <button        onClick={handleAddTask}>Add
Task</button>
    <ul>
      {tasks.map((task, index) => (
        <li key={index}>{task}</li>
      ))}
    </ul>
  </div>
);
};

export default ToDo;
```

Test for ToDo Component (ToDo.test.js):

Now, let's write tests for this component to ensure:

- The input field updates when a user types.
- Clicking the "Add Task" button adds the task to the list.
- The task appears in the list.

```javascript
import { render, screen, fireEvent } from '@testing-library/react';
import '@testing-library/jest-dom'; // For custom matchers
import ToDo from './ToDo';

test('renders ToDo component', () => {
  render(<ToDo />);

  // Test if the input field is in the document
  const inputField = screen.getByPlaceholderText('Add a task');
  expect(inputField).toBeInTheDocument();

  // Test if the button is in the document
  const button = screen.getByText('Add Task');
  expect(button).toBeInTheDocument();
});
```

255

```
test('adds task to the list', () => {
  render(<ToDo />);

  // Find the input field and button
  const                    inputField                    =
screen.getByPlaceholderText('Add a task');
  const button = screen.getByText('Add Task');

  // Type into the input field
  fireEvent.change(inputField,   {   target:   {
value: 'Learn React Testing' } });

  // Click the button to add the task
  fireEvent.click(button);

  // Test if the task appears in the list
  expect(screen.getByText('Learn           React
Testing')).toBeInTheDocument();
});

test('does not add empty tasks', () => {
  render(<ToDo />);

  // Find the button (without typing anything in
the input)
  const button = screen.getByText('Add Task');

  // Click the button to add an empty task
  fireEvent.click(button);
```

```
// Ensure the list is empty
expect(screen.queryByText('')).toBeNull();
});
```

Explanation of Tests:

1. **First Test (`renders ToDo component`)**:
   - This test checks if the input field and button are rendered correctly by using `screen.getByPlaceholderText` and `screen.getByText`.

2. **Second Test (`adds task to the list`)**:
   - This test checks if the user can add a task by typing into the input field and clicking the "Add Task" button.
   - `fireEvent.change` simulates typing in the input, and `fireEvent.click` simulates clicking the button.
   - The test then checks if the task appears in the list using `screen.getByText`.

3. **Third Test (`does not add empty tasks`)**:
   - This test ensures that clicking the "Add Task" button without entering any text does not add an empty task to the list.

Best Practices for Testing in React

1. **Test Behavior, Not Implementation**:
   - Focus on testing how the user interacts with the app and what the app should do, rather than how it is implemented. This leads to more maintainable and future-proof tests.

2. **Use Jest Matchers and React Testing Library Queries**:
   - Use `screen.getByText`, `screen.getByRole`, and other queries from React Testing Library to select elements based on user-facing properties (text content, accessibility roles, etc.).
   - Use `@testing-library/jest-dom` for extended matchers like `.toBeInTheDocument()` and `.toHaveClass()`.

3. **Keep Tests Isolated**:
   - Each test should test one thing in isolation. This makes it easier to diagnose issues when tests fail.

4. **Mocking and Spying**:
   - Use Jest's mocking capabilities (`jest.fn()`) to mock functions, modules, or timers that are not directly related to the component under test.

5. **Test User Interaction**:

o   Prefer testing user interactions using `fireEvent` or `user-event` rather than testing direct manipulation of the DOM.

Key Takeaways:

- **Unit Testing**: Tests individual components or functions in isolation, ensuring they work as expected.
- **Integration Testing**: Tests how multiple components or systems work together.
- **React Testing Library**: A tool that helps test React components by focusing on how users interact with the app rather than its implementation.
- **Jest**: A testing framework used to run tests, assert outcomes, and mock functions or modules.
- **Real-World Example**: We wrote tests for a simple To-Do list application, demonstrating how to test components for proper functionality, user interaction, and edge cases like empty inputs.

In the next chapter, we will explore **testing in Angular** and how to write unit and integration tests for Angular components, services, and more.

CHAPTER 22

TESTING IN ANGULAR

Setting Up Testing in Angular with Jasmine and Karma

Testing is a critical part of building robust applications, and Angular provides a comprehensive solution for testing with **Jasmine** (a behavior-driven testing framework) and **Karma** (a test runner). Together, they enable developers to write unit tests and run them in real-time, giving immediate feedback.

1. What are Jasmine and Karma?

- **Jasmine**: A popular JavaScript testing framework that allows you to write test cases in a human-readable format. It supports features like spies, mocks, assertions, and test suites.
- **Karma**: A test runner that works with various testing frameworks, including Jasmine. It runs tests in real browsers and provides a report of the test results.

Setting Up Testing with Angular CLI

When you create a new Angular project using the **Angular CLI**, Jasmine and Karma are automatically set up. However, if you want to manually set them up, follow these steps:

1. **Install Jasmine and Karma**: If Jasmine and Karma aren't already installed, you can install them using npm:

```bash
npm install --save-dev jasmine karma karma-jasmine karma-chrome-launcher
```

2. **Configure Karma**: Karma is configured through the `karma.conf.js` file. This file is created automatically when you use Angular CLI to set up the project. It includes settings like the test framework (Jasmine), the browser to run the tests in (Chrome), and which files to include in the test environment.

The `karma.conf.js` file should look something like this:

```javascript
module.exports = function(config) {
    config.set({
        basePath: '',
        frameworks: ['jasmine'],
        files: [
```

261

```
        'src/test.ts'
    ],
    browsers: ['Chrome'],
    reporters: ['progress'],
    singleRun: false,
    restartOnFileChange: true
    });
};
```

3. **Running Tests**: Once the setup is complete, you can run your tests using the following command:

```bash
ng test
```

This command will start Karma and execute your tests in a browser, displaying the results in the terminal or the browser console.

Writing Unit Tests for Angular Services and Components

Unit Testing Angular Services

A service in Angular is typically responsible for handling business logic or interacting with APIs. Writing unit tests for services is essential to ensure that the logic is correct and the services behave as expected.

Example: Testing an Angular Service

Let's create a simple **UserService** and write a test for it.

user.service.ts:

```typescript
import { Injectable } from '@angular/core';

@Injectable({
  providedIn: 'root'
})
export class UserService {
  getUser(id: number): string {
    return `User with ID: ${id}`;
  }
}
```

user.service.spec.ts (Unit Test):

```typescript
import { TestBed } from '@angular/core/testing';
import { UserService } from './user.service';

describe('UserService', () => {
```

```
let service: UserService;

beforeEach(() => {
  TestBed.configureTestingModule({});
  service = TestBed.inject(UserService);
});

it('should be created', () => {
  expect(service).toBeTruthy();
});

it('should return correct user by ID', () => {
  const userId = 1;
  const result = service.getUser(userId);
  expect(result).toBe(`User       with       ID:
${userId}`);
  });
});
```

In this test:

- **TestBed**: Configures the testing module and prepares the environment for testing.
- **beforeEach**: Runs before each test to set up the environment.
- **it**: Defines a test case. The first parameter is a description of the test, and the second is a function containing the test logic.

- **expect**: The Jasmine assertion function used to define what we expect the test outcome to be.

Key Points:

- Testing a service typically involves checking if the service methods return the expected results.
- Using Angular's **TestBed** allows for easy setup and initialization of the testing environment.

Unit Testing Angular Components

Components are the heart of Angular applications, and testing them ensures that they render correctly, handle user input, and interact with services as expected.

Example: Testing an Angular Component

Let's write a test for a simple **TodoComponent**.

todo.component.ts:

```typescript
import { Component } from '@angular/core';
import { TodoService } from '../todo.service';
```

```typescript
@Component({
  selector: 'app-todo',
  template: `
    <div>
      <h1>{{ title }}</h1>
      <ul>
        <li *ngFor="let todo of todos">{{ todo }}</li>
      </ul>
      <button (click)="addTodo()">Add Todo</button>
    </div>
  `
})
export class TodoComponent {
  title = 'Todo List';
  todos: string[] = [];

  constructor(private todoService: TodoService) {}

  addTodo() {
    this.todos.push('New Todo');
  }
}
```

todo.component.spec.ts (Unit Test):

typescript

```
import { ComponentFixture, TestBed } from
'@angular/core/testing';
import { TodoComponent } from './todo.component';
import { TodoService } from '../todo.service';

describe('TodoComponent', () => {
  let component: TodoComponent;
  let fixture: ComponentFixture<TodoComponent>;
  let todoService: TodoService;

  beforeEach(() => {
    TestBed.configureTestingModule({
      declarations: [ TodoComponent ],
      providers: [ TodoService ]
    });

    fixture                              =
TestBed.createComponent(TodoComponent);
    component = fixture.componentInstance;
    todoService = TestBed.inject(TodoService);
    fixture.detectChanges();
  });

  it('should create the component', () => {
    expect(component).toBeTruthy();
  });

  it('should add a todo item', () => {
    component.addTodo();
```

```
  expect(component.todos.length).toBe(1);
  expect(component.todos[0]).toBe('New Todo');
});


it('should display todo items in the template',
() => {
  component.addTodo();
  fixture.detectChanges();
  const compiled = fixture.nativeElement;

expect(compiled.querySelector('ul').textContent
).toContain('New Todo');
  });
});
```

In this test:

- **ComponentFixture**: Allows us to interact with the component and its template.
- **detectChanges()**: Triggers Angular's change detection cycle to update the component's view.
- **DOM Manipulation**: The test checks if the `todo` items are displayed correctly in the DOM using `fixture.nativeElement`.

Key Points:

- Component tests generally verify if the component renders correctly and behaves as expected.

- **DOM Testing**: You can test if elements appear or are updated in the DOM when interacting with the component.

Real-World Example: Test-Driven Development with Angular

Test-Driven Development (TDD) is an approach where you write tests before writing the actual code. This ensures that your application is designed with tests in mind and helps maintain a high level of code quality.

Let's walk through a **Test-Driven Development** approach for implementing a **simple calculator app**.

Step 1: Write the Test First

We start by writing tests for the features we want to implement.

1. **Create a Service for Calculator Logic**: The service will have methods for addition, subtraction, multiplication, and division.

   calculator.service.ts:

   ```typescript
   ```

269

```typescript
import { Injectable } from '@angular/core';

@Injectable({
  providedIn: 'root'
})
export class CalculatorService {
  add(a: number, b: number): number {
    return a + b;
  }

  subtract(a: number, b: number): number {
    return a - b;
  }

  multiply(a: number, b: number): number {
    return a * b;
  }

  divide(a: number, b: number): number {
    if (b === 0) {
      throw new Error('Division by zero');
    }
    return a / b;
  }
}
```

2. **Write Unit Tests**:

calculator.service.spec.ts:

270

```typescript
import { TestBed } from
'@angular/core/testing';
import { CalculatorService } from
'./calculator.service';

describe('CalculatorService', () => {
  let service: CalculatorService;

  beforeEach(() => {
    TestBed.configureTestingModule({});
    service =
TestBed.inject(CalculatorService);
  });

  it('should add two numbers', () => {
    expect(service.add(2, 3)).toBe(5);
  });

  it('should subtract two numbers', () =>
{
    expect(service.subtract(5,
3)).toBe(2);
  });

  it('should multiply two numbers', () =>
{
```

271

```
        expect(service.multiply(2,
3)).toBe(6);
    });

    it('should divide two numbers', () => {
        expect(service.divide(6, 3)).toBe(2);
    });

    it('should throw an error when dividing
by zero', () => {
        expect(()      =>      service.divide(5,
0)).toThrowError('Division by zero');
    });
});
```

Step 2: Implement the Code

Now that we have the tests, we implement the calculator logic. This was done in the `calculator.service.ts` file earlier. The tests should pass since we wrote them to match the expected behavior.

Step 3: Run the Tests

Finally, run the tests to ensure everything is working correctly:

```bash
ng test
```

All the tests should pass, confirming that our calculator logic works as expected.

Key Takeaways:

- **Jasmine**: The testing framework used in Angular for writing unit and integration tests.
- **Karma**: A test runner that works with Jasmine to execute tests in real-time in the browser.
- **Unit Testing Services**: Angular services are tested by checking their methods and ensuring they return the expected values.
- **Unit Testing Components**: Angular components are tested by checking their DOM behavior and interaction with the services.
- **Test-Driven Development (TDD)**: TDD helps ensure code is testable and encourages the creation of tests before writing the actual implementation.

In the next chapter, we will explore **End-to-End (E2E) Testing** in Angular with Protractor, focusing on how to test the entire application workflow.

CHAPTER 23

BUILDING PROGRESSIVE WEB APPS WITH REACT

What is a Progressive Web App (PWA)?

A **Progressive Web App (PWA)** is a type of web application that uses modern web technologies to provide a native app-like experience for users on the web. PWAs are designed to work on any device, offering features like offline functionality, push notifications, and fast loading times. They aim to deliver a seamless, engaging user experience regardless of the network conditions.

Key Characteristics of PWAs:

1. **Responsive**: PWAs are designed to fit on any screen size, from mobile phones to desktops.
2. **Offline Functionality**: PWAs can work offline or on low-quality networks by using service workers to cache resources and data.
3. **App-like Experience**: PWAs offer features like smooth animations, push notifications, and the ability to add the app to the home screen.

4. **Fast Loading**: PWAs are optimized for speed, providing fast loading times even in poor network conditions.

5. **Installation**: PWAs can be installed on the user's device without going through an app store, making them easy to distribute.

Benefits of PWAs:

- **Increased Engagement**: PWAs provide a native-like experience, encouraging users to spend more time on your app.

- **Improved Performance**: With features like caching and service workers, PWAs load quickly, even on slow networks.

- **Cross-Platform Compatibility**: PWAs work on all platforms, including iOS, Android, and desktop, without the need for separate native apps.

Setting Up a PWA with React

To convert a React app into a Progressive Web App, you need to make a few changes and configurations to enable key features like offline functionality, caching, and the ability to install the app.

Steps to Set Up a PWA with React:

1. **Create a New React App**: If you haven't already created a React app, you can start by using **Create React App** (CRA), which comes with built-in support for PWAs. Create a new React project:

bash

```
npx create-react-app my-pwa-app
cd my-pwa-app
```

2. **Enable PWA Features in Create React App**: Create React App comes with a service worker configuration that you can enable to make your app a PWA.

    o In the `src/index.js` file, change the service worker registration to `register()` instead of `unregister()`. By default, CRA disables service workers to avoid caching issues during development. To enable PWA functionality, modify the following:

javascript

```
import React from 'react';
import ReactDOM from 'react-dom';
import './index.css';
import App from './App';
import        reportWebVitals        from
'./reportWebVitals';
```

276

```
import * as serviceWorkerRegistration from
'./serviceWorkerRegistration';

ReactDOM.render(
  <React.StrictMode>
    <App />
  </React.StrictMode>,
  document.getElementById('root')
);


serviceWorkerRegistration.register();   //
Register the service worker to enable PWA
reportWebVitals();
```

By calling `serviceWorkerRegistration.register()`, you're telling the app to register the service worker, which allows the app to cache resources and work offline.

3. **Modify the `public/manifest.json` File**: The **manifest file** is essential for PWAs, as it defines the app's metadata and how it will behave when installed on a device (such as the name, icons, background color, etc.).

   Open the `public/manifest.json` file and update the fields as per your app's branding and requirements:

```
json
```

```json
{
  "short_name": "React PWA",
  "name": "My React Progressive Web App",
  "icons": [
    {
      "src": "favicon.ico",
      "sizes": "64x64 32x32 24x24 16x16",
      "type": "image/x-icon"
    }
  ],
  "start_url": ".",
  "display": "standalone",
  "background_color": "#ffffff",
  "theme_color": "#000000"
}
```

- o **short_name**: A short name for your app (used when the app is installed).
- o **name**: The full name of your app.
- o **start_url**: The URL to open when the app is launched (use . for the root).
- o **display**: Defines how the app is displayed when launched (set to standalone to make it look like a native app).
- o **background_color**: The background color of the splash screen when the app is launched.
- o **theme_color**: The color of the app's toolbar.

4. **Testing the PWA**: Once you've made the necessary updates, you can start the app by running:

```bash
```

```
npm start
```

Visit `http://localhost:3000` in your browser, and you should see your app running with basic PWA features.

To test the offline capabilities, open **DevTools** in Chrome, go to the **Application** tab, and check if the service worker is active. You can also simulate offline mode and refresh the page to ensure your app still works without an internet connection.

5. **Creating a Production Build**: To generate the production-ready PWA, you can build the app using the following command:

```bash
```

```
npm run build
```

This creates an optimized version of your app in the `build/` folder. You can deploy this folder to any static file server or hosting platform, like **Netlify**, **GitHub Pages**, or **Firebase Hosting**.

279

Real-World Example: Building a React-Based PWA

Let's build a simple **To-Do List PWA** that works offline and can be installed on a user's device.

Step-by-Step Process:

1. **Create a To-Do Component**: First, let's create a simple To-Do app component. We'll build functionality to add and remove tasks.

   TodoApp.js:

   ```javascript
   import React, { useState, useEffect } from 'react';

   const TodoApp = () => {
     const [tasks, setTasks] = useState([]);
     const [newTask, setNewTask] = useState('');

     useEffect(() => {
       const storedTasks = JSON.parse(localStorage.getItem('tasks'));
   ```

```
  if (storedTasks) {
    setTasks(storedTasks);
  }
}, []);

const addTask = () => {
  const    updatedTasks    =    [...tasks,
newTask];
    setTasks(updatedTasks);
    setNewTask('');
    localStorage.setItem('tasks',
JSON.stringify(updatedTasks));
  };

const removeTask = (taskToRemove) => {
  const            updatedTasks            =
tasks.filter((task)      =>      task      !==
taskToRemove);
    setTasks(updatedTasks);
    localStorage.setItem('tasks',
JSON.stringify(updatedTasks));
  };

return (
  <div>
    <h1>To-Do List</h1>
    <input
      type="text"
      value={newTask}
```

281

```
          onChange={(e)                    =>
setNewTask(e.target.value)}
          placeholder="Enter a new task"
        />
        <button        onClick={addTask}>Add
Task</button>
        <ul>
          {tasks.map((task, index) => (
            <li key={index}>
              {task}
              <button    onClick={()    =>
removeTask(task)}>Remove</button>
            </li>
          ))}
        </ul>
      </div>
    );
};

export default TodoApp;
```

2. **Updating the Manifest File**: Open the `public/manifest.json` file and ensure that it has the necessary details for your To-Do app.

```json
{
  "short_name": "To-Do App",
```

```
"name": "Progressive To-Do App",
"icons": [
  {
    "src": "favicon.ico",
    "sizes": "64x64 32x32 24x24 16x16",
    "type": "image/x-icon"
  }
],
"start_url": ".",
"display": "standalone",
"background_color": "#ffffff",
"theme_color": "#000000"
}
```

3. **Service Worker**: With the service worker now registered, the app will automatically cache the assets and work offline.

4. **Test the Offline Functionality**: After building the app, you can simulate offline behavior through the **Chrome Developer Tools**:

   o Open DevTools and go to the **Application** tab.

   o Under **Service Workers**, make sure the service worker is active.

   o Turn off the network to simulate offline mode and refresh the page. Your To-Do app should continue to work and show previously added tasks.

5. **PWA Installation**: When you visit the app in Chrome, you'll notice a prompt asking if you want to install the app. After installation, the app will be available as a PWA on your device's home screen, and you can access it like any other native app.

Key Takeaways:

- **PWAs** provide an app-like experience on the web, offering offline capabilities, fast loading, and the ability to install on a device.
- **Service Workers** are a key technology that enables offline functionality by caching assets and handling network requests.
- **React** makes it easy to build PWAs using **Create React App**, which provides built-in support for service workers and other PWA features.
- **Manifest File**: The manifest file defines the app's metadata and behavior when installed on a device.
- **Real-World Example**: We built a simple To-Do app that works offline and can be installed as a PWA on a device, demonstrating how to create and deploy a React-based Progressive Web App.

In the next chapter, we will explore **Deploying PWAs** to production environments and how to ensure your app works smoothly on different devices and platforms.

CHAPTER 24

BUILDING PROGRESSIVE WEB APPS WITH ANGULAR

Setting Up a PWA with Angular

A **Progressive Web App (PWA)** provides users with a seamless experience across devices and network conditions. In this chapter, we'll explore how to set up a PWA using **Angular**, a framework that has built-in support for building and optimizing Progressive Web Apps. Angular PWAs provide features like offline functionality, installation on the user's device, and faster loading, making them ideal for modern web development.

Steps to Set Up a PWA in Angular

1. **Create a New Angular Project**: If you don't have an Angular project yet, create a new one using the Angular CLI:

bash

```
ng new angular-pwa
cd angular-pwa
```

2. **Install Angular PWA Support**: Angular provides a simple way to add PWA support using the **@angular/pwa** package. This package adds a service worker to your application and makes the necessary configurations for PWA functionality.

To add PWA support, run the following command:

```bash
ng add @angular/pwa
```

This command modifies your application by:

- o Adding the `@angular/service-worker` package.
- o Creating or modifying the `ngsw-config.json` file, which contains configurations for the service worker.
- o Updating the `src/manifest.json` file to define the metadata of your PWA (icons, name, start URL, etc.).
- o Modifying the `src/index.html` file to include a link to the manifest file and a meta tag for the theme color.

3. **Configure the `manifest.json` File**: After running the `ng add @angular/pwa` command, Angular will automatically generate a `manifest.json` file in the

287

`src/` directory. This file contains important metadata about your app and is used when installing the PWA on devices.

The `manifest.json` file typically includes properties such as:

- o **name**: The full name of the application.
- o **short_name**: The shorter name of the app, used for the home screen.
- o **icons**: Icons that will be displayed on the device's home screen.
- o **background_color**: The background color for the splash screen when the app is launched.
- o **theme_color**: The color of the app's toolbar when it is running.

Example of `src/manifest.json`:

json

```
{
  "name": "Angular PWA",
  "short_name": "AngularPWA",
  "icons": [
    {
      "src":              "assets/icons/icon-192x192.png",
```

```json
      "sizes": "192x192",
      "type": "image/png"
    },
    {
      "src":              "assets/icons/icon-
512x512.png",
      "sizes": "512x512",
      "type": "image/png"
    }
  ],
  "start_url": ".",
  "display": "standalone",
  "background_color": "#ffffff",
  "theme_color": "#000000"
}
```

4. **Setting Up Service Workers**: A **service worker** is a script that runs in the background, separate from the web page, and helps manage caching, background sync, and push notifications. Service workers are key to PWAs because they allow apps to work offline.

   Angular uses the **Service Worker API** to cache assets and enable offline functionality. To enable service workers, open the `angular.json` file and ensure that the `"serviceWorker"` option is set to `true` for the production build configuration:

   json

```
"configurations": {
  "production": {
    "fileReplacements": [
      {
        "replace":
"src/environments/environment.ts",
        "with":
"src/environments/environment.prod.ts"
      }
    ],
    "serviceWorker": true,
    "optimization": true,
    "outputHashing": "all",
    "sourceMap": false,
    "extractCss": true,
    "namedChunks": false,
    "aot": true,
    "extractLicenses": true,
    "statsJson": false
  }
}
```

5. **Build the Project for Production**: Once everything is set up, build your Angular project for production:

```bash
bash

ng build --prod
```

290

This will create an optimized version of the app in the `dist/` folder. The service worker will automatically cache the app's assets, and the app will be ready to function as a PWA.

6. **Test the PWA**: You can test your Angular PWA by serving it locally with a simple HTTP server:

bash

```
npm install -g http-server
http-server ./dist/angular-pwa
```

Open `http://localhost:8080` in your browser, and you should see the app running as a PWA. You can also use Chrome's DevTools to simulate offline behavior and test the caching mechanism.

Best Practices for Building Offline-First Web Apps

Building a reliable **offline-first** web app is one of the core principles of creating a successful PWA. Here are some best practices to follow:

1. **Cache Essential Assets**: Use the service worker to cache critical assets like HTML, CSS, JavaScript files, and

291

images. This ensures that users can access the app even without an internet connection.

2. **Use Cache Strategies**: Implement different cache strategies for different resources. For example:

   o Cache static assets like images and JavaScript files.

   o Use network-first strategies for data that needs to be up-to-date, such as API responses.

3. **Handle Network Failures Gracefully**: Ensure that the app can handle network failures gracefully. If the user is offline, provide a meaningful offline experience, such as showing a cached version of the data or a custom offline page.

4. **Optimize for Performance**: PWAs need to load quickly. Optimize the app's performance by:

   o Reducing the size of the app's assets (minifying JavaScript and CSS, lazy-loading resources).

   o Using service workers to cache assets and ensure fast loading times, even on slow networks.

5. **Test Offline Functionality**: Regularly test your PWA in different network conditions. Use browser developer tools to simulate offline scenarios and make sure the app continues to work without an internet connection.

6. **Use Push Notifications**: Implement push notifications to engage users even when they are not actively using the

app. PWAs can show push notifications using the Push API and Notification API.

Real-World Example: Creating a PWA with Angular

Let's build a simple **To-Do List PWA** that allows users to add, view, and delete tasks, and works offline.

Step 1: Set Up the Angular Project

Create a new Angular project and set it up as a PWA:

bash

```
ng new todo-pwa
cd todo-pwa
ng add @angular/pwa
```

Step 2: Modify the To-Do Component

Create a To-Do component to handle adding and displaying tasks.

todo.component.ts:

typescript

```
import { Component } from '@angular/core';
```

```
@Component({
  selector: 'app-todo',
  templateUrl: './todo.component.html',
  styleUrls: ['./todo.component.css']
})
export class TodoComponent {
  task: string = '';
  tasks: string[] = [];

  addTask() {
    if (this.task) {
      this.tasks.push(this.task);
      this.task = '';
    }
  }

  removeTask(task: string) {
    this.tasks = this.tasks.filter(t => t !==
task);
  }
}
```

todo.component.html:

```
html
```

```
<div>
  <h1>To-Do List</h1>
```

```
<input [(ngModel)]="task" placeholder="Enter a new task" />
<button (click)="addTask()">Add Task</button>
<ul>
  <li *ngFor="let task of tasks">
    {{ task }}
    <button (click)="removeTask(task)">Delete</button>
  </li>
</ul>
</div>
```

Step 3: Add the Component to the App

In `app.module.ts`, import the necessary modules and declare the component:

typescript

```typescript
import { NgModule } from '@angular/core';
import { BrowserModule } from '@angular/platform-browser';
import { FormsModule } from '@angular/forms';
import { AppComponent } from './app.component';
import { TodoComponent } from './todo/todo.component';

@NgModule({
  declarations: [AppComponent, TodoComponent],
```

```
  imports: [BrowserModule, FormsModule],
  providers: [],
  bootstrap: [AppComponent]
})
export class AppModule {}
```

Step 4: Test the PWA

After building the app for production, you can test it by serving the `dist/` folder with a static server:

```
bash
```

```
ng build --prod
http-server ./dist/todo-pwa
```

Open `http://localhost:8080` in your browser, and you should see the To-Do List app working as a PWA. Try testing it by going offline (simulated through DevTools) and confirming that the app still works.

Key Takeaways:

- **PWAs** are web applications that provide native app-like experiences using modern web technologies, including service workers and caching.

- **Angular** makes it easy to turn an app into a PWA by using the Angular CLI, which adds built-in support for service workers and manifests.

- **Offline-First Web Apps**: Cache critical assets, handle network failures gracefully, and ensure that the app is responsive and fast even without a network connection.

- **Real-World Example**: We built a simple To-Do List app with Angular, demonstrating how to set up a PWA, implement offline functionality, and test the app in different network conditions.

In the next chapter, we will discuss **Deploying PWAs** to production environments, covering hosting platforms and strategies to ensure optimal performance across devices.

CHAPTER 25

PERFORMANCE OPTIMIZATION IN REACT AND ANGULAR

Optimizing App Performance: Code Splitting, Lazy Loading, and Caching

Performance optimization is crucial to delivering fast, responsive applications. Both **React** and **Angular** provide built-in tools and techniques for optimizing app performance. In this chapter, we will cover key techniques such as **code splitting**, **lazy loading**, and **caching** to help you improve the speed and overall user experience of your web applications.

1. Code Splitting

Code splitting is the process of dividing your app's JavaScript code into smaller bundles that can be loaded on demand rather than all at once. This technique helps reduce the initial load time of your app, as only the required code is loaded when needed.

React: Code Splitting with React.lazy()

In React, **React.lazy()** and **Suspense** allow you to implement code splitting at the component level. This means that only the components that are needed are loaded, rather than loading the entire bundle upfront.

- **React.lazy()** allows you to dynamically import a component when it is needed.
- **Suspense** provides a loading state while the component is being loaded asynchronously.

Here's an example of how you can implement code splitting in React:

javascript

```
import React, { Suspense } from 'react';

// Dynamically import the component
const LazyComponent = React.lazy(() =>
import('./LazyComponent'));

function App() {
  return (
    <div>
      <h1>React Code Splitting Example</h1>
      {/* Suspense handles loading state while
the component is being loaded */}
```

```
    <Suspense
fallback={<div>Loading...</div>}>
        <LazyComponent />
    </Suspense>
  </div>
 );
}

export default App;
```

In this example, **LazyComponent** will only be loaded when it is needed, reducing the initial bundle size.

Angular: Lazy Loading Modules

In Angular, **lazy loading** is implemented at the module level, meaning entire feature modules are only loaded when the user navigates to a particular route.

To set up lazy loading in Angular:

1. **Create a Feature Module**: You can generate a feature module using the Angular CLI:

    ```bash
    bash

    ng generate module feature
    ```

2. **Set Up Routing for Lazy Loading**: In the main app routing module (`app-routing.module.ts`), configure lazy loading for the feature module.

```typescript
const routes: Routes = [
  {
    path: 'feature',
    loadChildren:          ()              =>
import('./feature/feature.module').then(m
=> m.FeatureModule)
  }
];
```

This ensures that the **FeatureModule** is only loaded when the user navigates to the /feature path, reducing the initial load time of the application.

2. Lazy Loading

Lazy loading is a performance optimization technique where you delay the loading of certain resources or components until they are needed. This can significantly improve the perceived performance of your application by reducing the time it takes to load the initial page.

React: Lazy Loading Images

React doesn't have built-in support for lazy loading images, but you can implement it using the **Intersection Observer API** or third-party libraries like **react-lazyload**.

Here's an example of lazy loading images with **React.lazy()** and **Suspense**:

```javascript
import React, { Suspense } from 'react';

const LazyImage = React.lazy(() => import('./LazyImage'));

function App() {
  return (
    <div>
      <Suspense fallback={<div>Loading image...</div>}>
        <LazyImage src="image.jpg" />
      </Suspense>
    </div>
  );
}

export default App;
```

This approach delays the loading of images until they are about to enter the viewport.

Angular: Lazy Loading Modules and Components

Angular supports lazy loading both at the **module** and **component** level. As shown earlier, lazy loading modules can improve the initial loading performance.

To implement lazy loading at the component level, you can use **Angular's `loadChildren` method** and **dynamic component loading**.

typescript

```
import { Component, ViewChild, ViewContainerRef,
ComponentFactoryResolver } from '@angular/core';
import { MyComponent } from './my.component';

@Component({
  selector: 'app-root',
  template:    `<ng-template    #container></ng-
template>`
})
export class AppComponent {
  @ViewChild('container',        {        read:
ViewContainerRef, static: true }) container;
```

```
  constructor(private                    resolver:
ComponentFactoryResolver) {}

  loadComponent() {
    const                factory              =
this.resolver.resolveComponentFactory(MyCompone
nt);
    this.container.createComponent(factory);
  }
}
```

In this example, `MyComponent` will only be loaded when the `loadComponent()` method is called, saving initial load time.

3. Caching

Caching is a powerful technique for improving performance by storing frequently accessed data or assets in the browser, so they don't need to be requested from the server repeatedly.

React: Service Worker Caching

React PWAs use **service workers** to cache assets and API responses, enabling offline functionality and faster load times. Service workers can be configured using **Workbox**, a set of libraries that makes it easier to manage caching.

To set up caching in a React PWA, first ensure that you have a service worker registered (this is handled by `create-react-app` when adding PWA support). Then, you can configure caching strategies for different types of assets.

Angular: Service Worker Caching

Angular's service worker setup uses **Angular Service Worker** and **@angular/service-worker** to provide caching capabilities. Once you add PWA support to an Angular app, it automatically configures a service worker and caching strategies.

In the `ngsw-config.json` file, you can define which assets to cache and how to handle them. For example:

```json
{
  "assetGroups": [
    {
      "name": "core",
      "installMode": "prefetch",
      "updateMode": "prefetch",
      "resources": {
        "files": [
          "/index.html",
          "/favicon.ico",
          "/assets/**",
          "/styles.css"
```

```
        ]
      }
    }
  ]
}
```

This configuration will cache assets like `index.html`, images, and stylesheets so they can be served offline.

Best Practices for Improving App Speed and User Experience

1. Optimize Bundle Size

- **Code Splitting**: Split your JavaScript files to load only the necessary code when needed.
- **Tree Shaking**: Eliminate unused code from your bundle. Both Angular and React support tree shaking out of the box.
- **Minification**: Use tools like **Terser** to minify JavaScript, reducing the file size.

2. Efficient Asset Management

- **Lazy Loading**: Implement lazy loading for images, components, and routes to delay loading until needed.

- **Optimize Images**: Compress images and use modern formats like **WebP** to reduce their size without losing quality.

3. Caching and Service Workers

- **Service Workers**: Use service workers to cache assets and data, enabling offline access and faster loading.
- **HTTP Caching**: Leverage HTTP caching for static assets and API responses.

4. Avoid Blocking JavaScript

- **Defer non-essential JavaScript**: Use the `async` and `defer` attributes for non-critical JavaScript to prevent it from blocking page rendering.
- **Lazy Load Scripts**: Lazy load external libraries and scripts to reduce the initial loading time.

5. Optimize Rendering

- **Virtual DOM (React)**: React's virtual DOM ensures that only the necessary updates are made, minimizing re-rendering.
- **Change Detection (Angular)**: Angular's change detection mechanism can be optimized using **OnPush** strategy to limit the number of checks.

6. Minimize Reflows and Repaints

- **Batch DOM Manipulation**: Minimize DOM manipulations by batching them together to avoid unnecessary reflows and repaints in the browser.
- **CSS Optimization**: Use efficient CSS selectors and avoid unnecessary styles that impact rendering performance.

Real-World Example: Performance Tuning for React and Angular Apps

Let's apply performance optimization techniques to a **To-Do List App** built with React and Angular.

React App Performance Tuning

1. **Code Splitting with React.lazy()**: We can use React.lazy() to load the To-Do item component only when it's needed. This reduces the initial bundle size.

   javascript

   ```javascript
   const TodoItem = React.lazy(() =>
   import('./TodoItem'));
   ```

308

2. **Service Worker Caching**: By using a service worker, we can cache the app's static assets, making the app load faster on subsequent visits.

3. **Memoization with React.memo**: We can use `React.memo` to prevent unnecessary re-renders of components that receive the same props.

```javascript
const TodoItem = React.memo(({ task }) =>
<div>{task}</div>);
```

4. **Avoid Inline Functions**: Inline functions in JSX can cause unnecessary re-renders. Instead, define them outside the JSX or use `useCallback` to memoize them.

Angular App Performance Tuning

1. **Lazy Loading Modules**: We can implement lazy loading for the To-Do feature module, so that it is only loaded when the user navigates to the corresponding route.

2. **Service Worker Caching**: The Angular PWA setup includes automatic caching of assets using Angular's **service worker** configuration.

3. **OnPush Change Detection**: By using the `OnPush` change detection strategy, Angular will only check for

changes when the input to a component changes, improving performance.

typescript

```
@Component({
  selector: 'app-todo-item',
  changeDetection:
ChangeDetectionStrategy.OnPush,
  template: '<div>{{ todo }}</div>'
})
```

4. **Track By in ngFor**: When rendering lists with `ngFor`, use `trackBy` to minimize DOM updates by tracking items by their unique identifiers.

html

```
<div *ngFor="let todo of todos; trackBy:
trackById">
  {{ todo.task }}
</div>
```
typescript

```
trackById(index, todo) {
  return todo.id;
}
```

Key Takeaways:

- **Code Splitting**: Break your app into smaller bundles to load only the necessary code, improving load times.
- **Lazy Loading**: Load resources, components, or routes only when they are required to improve initial load performance.
- **Caching**: Implement caching through service workers to improve performance and provide offline functionality.
- **Performance Best Practices**: Use lazy loading, optimize images, and take advantage of memoization, efficient CSS, and minimized DOM manipulations to ensure fast and smooth performance.
- **Real-World Tuning**: Both React and Angular have specific techniques for optimizing performance. By applying these methods, you can significantly enhance the speed and user experience of your app.

In the next chapter, we will dive into **Deploying React and Angular Applications**, exploring best practices for deploying optimized applications to production.

CHAPTER 26

SECURITY BEST PRACTICES IN JAVASCRIPT FRAMEWORKS

Understanding Common Security Threats (XSS, CSRF, etc.)

Web security is a critical aspect of modern web application development. Understanding common threats and implementing proper security measures ensures that your applications are safe and reliable. Below are the most common security threats developers face while building web applications.

1. Cross-Site Scripting (XSS)

XSS is a vulnerability that allows attackers to inject malicious scripts into web pages viewed by other users. These malicious scripts can execute in the user's browser and steal sensitive data, such as session cookies, or perform actions on behalf of the user without their consent.

Types of XSS:

- **Stored XSS**: Malicious scripts are stored on the server (e.g., in a database) and are later executed when the user views the page.
- **Reflected XSS**: Malicious scripts are reflected off the server and executed immediately when a user clicks on a malicious link.
- **DOM-based XSS**: Occurs when the browser's Document Object Model (DOM) is manipulated by malicious scripts, usually via URL manipulation or third-party scripts.

2. Cross-Site Request Forgery (CSRF)

CSRF is an attack where a malicious user tricks the victim into performing actions they didn't intend to, such as submitting a form or making a request that changes the state of the application. This often happens without the victim's knowledge, making it dangerous for applications that don't verify the authenticity of requests.

For example, a user could be tricked into submitting a form to transfer money or change account settings while being logged into a legitimate site.

3. SQL Injection (SQLi)

SQL Injection occurs when an attacker injects malicious SQL code into a query to manipulate the database. This can lead to unauthorized access to sensitive data, such as user credentials or private information.

4. Insecure Direct Object References (IDOR)

IDOR occurs when an attacker is able to access or manipulate objects (such as files or database records) that they should not have access to, typically by manipulating the URL or request parameters.

Implementing Security Measures in React and Angular

Both **React** and **Angular** provide features and guidelines to mitigate security risks, but it's important to follow best practices to ensure your applications are secure. Let's explore how to implement security measures in these frameworks to prevent common vulnerabilities.

React Security Best Practices

1. Preventing XSS in React

React is designed with security in mind. By default, React escapes any user input before rendering it to the DOM, which helps prevent XSS attacks. However, it's still important to follow these guidelines:

- **Avoid dangerouslySetInnerHTML**: React provides a `dangerouslySetInnerHTML` property that allows you to insert HTML directly into a component, which can be dangerous if the HTML comes from an untrusted source. Avoid using this property whenever possible, and sanitize any HTML before using it.

  ```javascript
  // Dangerous
  <div dangerouslySetInnerHTML={{ __html: userInput }} />

  // Safe: Use proper sanitization libraries
  // like DOMPurify if you need to insert raw
  // HTML
  ```

- **Sanitize User Input**: When accepting user input (such as comments or form fields), sanitize it before rendering it in your app. You can use libraries like **DOMPurify** or **sanitize-html** to remove potentially dangerous content.

  ```javascript
  import DOMPurify from 'dompurify';
  ```

315

```
const                    sanitizedHtml                    =
DOMPurify.sanitize(userInput);
```

2. Preventing CSRF in React

To prevent CSRF, it's essential to use anti-CSRF tokens or ensure that requests made by the app are only valid if they come from the same origin. You can use libraries like **axios** for sending requests with a token in the headers.

- **Set Up a CSRF Token**: When interacting with a server that requires authentication, ensure that all requests include a **CSRF token**. This token is generated on the server and added to the request headers.

```javascript
import axios from 'axios';

axios.defaults.headers.common['X-CSRF-Token'] = csrfToken;
```

3. Secure Authentication

- **JWT (JSON Web Tokens)**: JWT tokens are commonly used to handle user authentication in React apps. Always use **HTTPS** when transmitting JWT tokens and store them securely (preferably in HTTPOnly cookies).

```javascript
```

316

```
// Sending JWT token in HTTPOnly cookie for
enhanced security
document.cookie    =    `token=${jwtToken};
HttpOnly; Secure;`;
```

Angular Security Best Practices

1. Preventing XSS in Angular

Angular automatically sanitizes potentially dangerous content and prevents XSS attacks by using its **DomSanitizer**. This is especially useful when you're dealing with untrusted input, such as HTML content from a user.

- **Sanitize HTML Input**: If you need to insert HTML into your Angular components, use Angular's DomSanitizer to sanitize the HTML content.

```typescript
import { DomSanitizer, SafeHtml } from
'@angular/platform-browser';

constructor(private            sanitizer:
DomSanitizer) {}

public    sanitizeHtml(input:    string):
SafeHtml {
```

```
    return
this.sanitizer.bypassSecurityTrustHtml(in
put);
    }
```

2. Preventing CSRF in Angular

Angular provides built-in support for preventing CSRF attacks by automatically including the CSRF token in HTTP requests if the token is included in the response from the server.

- **Use Angular HttpClient**: Ensure that your server is sending the CSRF token in the headers, and Angular will include it in future requests automatically.

```typescript
import { HttpClient, HttpHeaders } from
'@angular/common/http';

const headers = new HttpHeaders().set('X-
CSRF-Token', csrfToken);
this.httpClient.get('/api/protected',    {
headers });
```

3. Secure Authentication with JWT

Like in React, JWT is commonly used for handling authentication in Angular apps. When sending JWT tokens, always store them securely and use **HTTPS** for secure transmission.

- **Store JWT in Secure Storage**: For added security, it's recommended to store JWT tokens in **HTTPOnly cookies** to prevent access from JavaScript. You can use Angular's `HttpClient` to send authenticated requests.

Real-World Example: Securing a Web App with JWT Authentication

Let's consider building a **To-Do List** app where users need to authenticate using JWT tokens. This will demonstrate securing a React or Angular app with JWT authentication and implementing best practices for securing APIs.

Step 1: Setting Up JWT Authentication on the Server

You'll need to set up JWT authentication on your server. Here's a simple example using **Node.js and Express** to handle authentication.

javascript

```javascript
const jwt = require('jsonwebtoken');
const express = require('express');
const app = express();
const secretKey = 'your-secret-key';
```

```javascript
// Middleware to verify JWT token
const authenticateJWT = (req, res, next) => {
  const                token                =
req.header('Authorization').split(' ')[1];
  if (!token) {
    return res.sendStatus(403);
  }

  jwt.verify(token, secretKey, (err, user) => {
    if (err) {
      return res.sendStatus(403);
    }
    req.user = user;
    next();
  });
};

// Login route to generate a token
app.post('/login', (req, res) => {
  const { username, password } = req.body;
  // Authenticate user (usually by checking in a
database)
  if (username === 'user' && password ===
'password') {
    const accessToken = jwt.sign({ username },
secretKey);
    res.json({ accessToken });
  } else {
```

320

```
    res.send('Username or password incorrect');
  }
});


// Protected route (only accessible with JWT)
app.get('/protected',  authenticateJWT,  (req,
res) => {
  res.json({ message: 'Protected data', user:
req.user });
});


app.listen(5000, () => {
  console.log('Server running on port 5000');
});
```

Step 2: Securing the Front-End (React Example)

In your React app, you can authenticate the user and store the JWT token securely (e.g., in an **HTTPOnly cookie**).

React - Login and Fetch Data:

1. **Login and Save JWT**: On the login page, once the user submits their credentials, call the API to get the JWT and store it securely.

   ```
   javascript
   ```

```javascript
const login = async (username, password) =>
{
  const       response       =       await
fetch('http://localhost:5000/login', {
    method: 'POST',
    body:    JSON.stringify({    username,
password }),
    headers:        {       'Content-Type':
'application/json' },
  });
  const data = await response.json();
  document.cookie                         =
`token=${data.accessToken};       HttpOnly;
Secure;`;
};
```

2. **Access Protected Data**: To access protected resources, send the JWT token in the request header.

```javascript
javascript

const fetchData = async () => {
  const              token              =
document.cookie.split('=')[1];
  const       response       =       await
fetch('http://localhost:5000/protected', {
    method: 'GET',
    headers: {
      Authorization: `Bearer ${token}`,
    },
```

```
  });
  const data = await response.json();
  console.log(data);
};
```

Step 3: Securing the Front-End (Angular Example)

In Angular, you can follow similar steps to store and use the JWT token.

1. **Login and Store JWT**: When the user logs in, store the JWT token in an **HTTPOnly cookie** for secure storage.

```typescript
login(username: string, password: string)
{
  return
this.httpClient.post('http://localhost:50
00/login', { username, password })
    .pipe(
      tap((response: any) => {
        document.cookie                =
`token=${response.accessToken}; HttpOnly;
Secure;`;
      })
    );
}
```

2. **Access Protected Data**: When making requests to a protected route, send the JWT token in the **Authorization** header.

```typescript
getProtectedData() {
  const             token             =
document.cookie.split('=')[1];
  return
this.httpClient.get('http://localhost:500
0/protected', {
    headers:                          new
HttpHeaders().set('Authorization', `Bearer
${token}`)
  });
}
```

Key Takeaways:

-   **XSS** and **CSRF** are common security threats in web applications. React and Angular provide best practices for mitigating these risks, such as using **input sanitization**, **CSRF tokens**, and **service workers** for secure API calls.
-   **JWT Authentication** provides a secure method for managing user sessions, and can be implemented in both React and Angular apps. Always store JWT tokens in

HTTPOnly cookies and use **HTTPS** for secure transmission.

- **Security Best Practices**:
  - Prevent **XSS** by sanitizing user input.
  - Protect against **CSRF** by using tokens and ensuring requests are made from trusted sources.
  - Use **JWT** for secure authentication and authorization, storing tokens securely.

In the next chapter, we will explore **Performance Monitoring** and **Logging** for React and Angular apps to ensure they remain fast and reliable in production.

CHAPTER 27

FUTURE TRENDS IN JAVASCRIPT FRAMEWORKS

Emerging Trends in JavaScript Frameworks

The landscape of JavaScript frameworks has evolved rapidly over the past decade, with frameworks like React, Angular, and Vue.js dominating the web development ecosystem. As technology continues to advance, new trends emerge that reshape the way developers build web applications. In this chapter, we will explore some of the key emerging trends in JavaScript frameworks, the future of popular frameworks like React and Angular, and how developers can keep their web apps up to date with these evolving technologies.

1. Server-Side Rendering (SSR) and Static Site Generation (SSG)

In recent years, **server-side rendering (SSR)** and **static site generation (SSG)** have gained popularity, particularly for improving SEO and performance. These techniques involve rendering web pages on the server before they reach the client, rather than rendering everything client-side.

Server-Side Rendering (SSR)

- **What it is**: With SSR, web pages are rendered on the server and sent as fully rendered HTML to the browser, which results in faster initial page loads and better SEO performance.
- **Why it's important**: It provides a significant performance boost for SEO, as search engines can easily index the content without relying on JavaScript execution.
- **Popular frameworks**: **Next.js** for React, **Nuxt.js** for Vue, and **Angular Universal** for Angular are some of the leading solutions for SSR.

Static Site Generation (SSG)

- **What it is**: SSG involves generating static HTML files at build time, rather than on-demand. This allows for extremely fast load times and improved performance, as pages are pre-built and served as static content.
- **Why it's important**: Static sites are faster, more secure (less server-side processing), and easier to deploy on content delivery networks (CDNs).

- **Popular frameworks**: **Next.js** (for React), **Nuxt.js** (for Vue), and **Gatsby** (for React) are popular tools that support SSG.

2. Jamstack Architecture

Jamstack stands for **JavaScript, APIs, and Markup**, which represents a modern architecture designed to deliver faster, more secure, and scalable websites. The Jamstack approach focuses on decoupling the front-end from the back-end, with APIs and pre-built static content handling dynamic functionality.

Benefits of Jamstack:

- **Speed**: Since content is served as static files, websites built using Jamstack can load faster.
- **Security**: Static sites have a smaller attack surface, as there's no dynamic server-side processing involved.
- **Scalability**: Jamstack applications can be easily scaled by distributing the static content across CDNs.

Popular tools like **Next.js**, **Gatsby**, and **Nuxt.js** align with Jamstack principles, helping developers create static websites that are highly dynamic and interactive.

3. Component-Driven Development (CDD)

Component-Driven Development (CDD) is a methodology where developers focus on creating and assembling individual UI components rather than building entire pages or views at once. This approach has gained traction due to the rise of component-based libraries and frameworks like **React**, **Vue**, and **Angular**.

Why CDD is Important:

- **Reusability**: Components are modular, reusable, and easy to manage, which leads to improved productivity and consistency across the application.
- **Maintainability**: By breaking down complex UI elements into smaller components, it's easier to manage and update code.
- **Design Systems**: Many companies are moving towards design systems, which are based on reusable components, making the design and development process more efficient.

Tools like **Storybook** help developers build and document UI components in isolation, making CDD an even more powerful approach.

4. Progressive Web Apps (PWAs)

Progressive Web Apps (PWAs) continue to be an important trend as they offer native app-like experiences using web

329

technologies. PWAs are increasingly seen as the future of mobile web development because they provide many of the benefits of native apps without requiring an app store download.

Why PWAs are important:

- **Offline capabilities**: PWAs can work offline, allowing users to interact with the app even when they have no internet connection.
- **Push notifications**: PWAs can send push notifications to users, keeping them engaged even when they aren't using the app.
- **App-like experience**: PWAs can be added to the home screen and accessed like native apps, providing a seamless user experience across devices.

Frameworks like **React**, **Angular**, and **Vue** all support PWA features out of the box, allowing developers to easily turn their apps into PWAs.

5. WebAssembly (Wasm)

WebAssembly (Wasm) is a low-level bytecode format that allows code written in multiple languages (like C, C++, Rust, etc.) to be run in the browser. This provides near-native performance for web applications and allows developers to run code that was previously only possible in desktop applications.

Why Wasm is Important:

- **Performance boost**: WebAssembly allows heavy computation tasks (such as image processing, 3D rendering, etc.) to be handled in the browser at near-native speeds.
- **Language flexibility**: Wasm enables developers to write parts of their applications in languages like C, C++, and Rust and still run them in the browser alongside JavaScript.

Although WebAssembly is still evolving, it has great potential to revolutionize the way we build web applications, especially in areas like gaming, media, and complex data processing.

The Future of React, Angular, and Other Popular Frameworks

As JavaScript frameworks continue to evolve, the future of **React**, **Angular**, and **Vue** is shaped by new features, community demands, and the growing ecosystem around them. Let's explore the direction these frameworks are headed:

React: The Rise of Concurrent Mode and Suspense

React has remained one of the most popular frameworks due to its flexibility, simplicity, and vibrant ecosystem. Moving forward, **React Concurrent Mode** and **Suspense** are key features that promise to enhance the performance and user experience:

- **Concurrent Mode**: Allows React to work on multiple tasks simultaneously, prioritizing important updates and improving app responsiveness.
- **Suspense**: React Suspense is designed for asynchronous rendering, allowing developers to manage code splitting, data fetching, and lazy loading more effectively.

React is also increasingly becoming a central tool for building PWAs and mobile applications, particularly with **React Native**.

Angular: Embracing Ivy and the Modular Future

Angular continues to be the go-to choice for building enterprise-scale applications. The introduction of the **Ivy rendering engine** has significantly improved Angular's performance and reduced bundle sizes. Angular's future is centered on:

- **Ivy**: The new compiler and runtime that will continue to improve performance, tree-shaking, and bundle sizes.
- **Modularization**: Angular is becoming even more modular with the introduction of **standalone**

components, allowing for better flexibility and easier app scaling.

Angular is also doubling down on **TypeScript**, ensuring a strongly-typed experience for developers, which helps in maintaining large-scale applications.

Vue: Growth and Ecosystem Expansion

Vue has become one of the most loved frameworks in the JavaScript community due to its simplicity, flexibility, and ease of integration with other technologies. Vue's future looks promising with:

- **Vue 3**: The introduction of Vue 3 brought **Composition API**, which offers better logic reuse and more flexibility for developers. Vue 3's enhanced performance, smaller size, and better TypeScript integration make it even more attractive for building modern apps.
- **Vuex 5**: Vuex, Vue's state management solution, will continue evolving, ensuring better scalability and simpler patterns for handling state in large applications.
- **Full-stack Development**: With **Nuxt.js**, Vue is increasingly being used for full-stack applications, offering powerful SSR and SSG features for building optimized web apps.

Vue's lightweight nature and flexibility will keep it relevant for building scalable, performant applications.

Real-World Example: Keeping Your Web App Up to Date with Evolving Technologies

Let's look at a **real-world example** of a web app built with **React** and **Angular**, focusing on keeping the app up to date with the latest features, performance optimizations, and security measures.

Example 1: React-based Web App (E-commerce Platform)

Imagine you're working on an e-commerce platform built with **React**. Here's how you can keep your app up to date:

1. **Code Splitting and Suspense**: As your app grows, you implement **code splitting** to ensure fast initial loads. You also use **Suspense** to improve how your app handles asynchronous data fetching.
2. **PWA Features**: By turning your app into a **PWA**, users can access the app offline and receive push notifications about new sales or promotions.
3. **Concurrent Mode**: With React's **Concurrent Mode**, you improve the responsiveness of your app by allowing React to handle UI updates in a more prioritized manner.

Example 2: Angular-based Web App (Internal Dashboard)

For an **internal dashboard** built with **Angular**, here's how you stay up to date with the latest technologies:

1. **Ivy**: The **Ivy rendering engine** ensures that your app performs optimally and loads faster, reducing the size of your bundles.

2. **Modularization**: By using **standalone components** and implementing lazy loading, you keep your app modular, reducing the amount of code that needs to be loaded initially.

3. **Security Enhancements**: With Angular's **HttpClient** and built-in support for **CSRF tokens**, you ensure that your app communicates securely with your back-end services.

In both cases, regularly upgrading your dependencies and testing your app in different environments ensures it remains up-to-date with the latest trends and technologies.

Key Takeaways:

- **Emerging Trends**: Key trends in JavaScript frameworks include **SSR**, **SSG**, **Jamstack**, **component-driven development**, **PWAs**, and **WebAssembly**. These trends improve the performance, scalability, and user experience of web applications.

- **The Future of Frameworks**:
  - **React** is focusing on **Concurrent Mode** and **Suspense** to improve performance and user interaction.
  - **Angular** is embracing the **Ivy rendering engine** and **modularization** for better performance and scalability.
  - **Vue** continues to grow with the **Composition API**, **Vuex 5**, and increased use in **full-stack development**.

- **Keeping Apps Up to Date**: Regularly adopting new features, performance optimizations, and security best practices ensures your web app stays relevant and efficient in an ever-evolving ecosystem.

In the next chapter, we will explore **Continuous Integration and Deployment (CI/CD)** practices for React and Angular apps, helping you automate the build, testing, and deployment process for faster releases.

www.ingramcontent.com/pod-product-compliance
Lightning Source LLC
LaVergne TN
LVHW051430050326
832903LV00030B/3008